MARINE SPECIAL WARFARE & ELITE UNIT TACTICS

BOB NEWMAN

PALADIN PRESS • BOULDER, COLORADO

D0721740

Marine Special Warfare and Elite Unit Tactics
by Bob Newman

Copyright © 1995 by Bob Newman

ISBN 0-87364-845-5
Printed in the United States of America

Published by Paladin Press, a division of
Paladin Enterprises, Inc., P.O. Box 1307,
Boulder, Colorado 80306, USA.
(303) 443-7250

Direct inquiries and/or orders to the above address.

PALADIN, PALADIN PRESS, and the "horse head" design
are trademarks belonging to Paladin Enterprises and
registered in United States Patent and Trademark Office.

Illustrations by Susan Newman

Visit our Web site at www.paladin-press.com

Contents

To the Marines who made the ultimate
sacrifice so that their brothers might live.

Acknowledgments

o book, especially one of this nature, can truly be written by one man, for the thoughts of fighters ranging from Sun Tzu and Napoleon to Rex Applegate and Fighting Joe Hooker have shaped these words and opinions. So for all those warfighters, tacticians, strategists, and leaders who went before me and wrote down their thoughts and ideas, thank you.

Jon Ford, my editor, pestered me until I got off my butt and did what I told him I would do.

My first platoon commander, 1st Lt.

Timothy A. Sloan, USMC, gave me some advice one day. "Be bold," he said. Sound advice, indeed.

My first platoon sergeant, then SSgt. C.T. Garr, USMC, now a sergeant major, saw enough rough potential in me to polish me up. Thanks, sergeant major.

Col. J.L. Clark, USMC, LtCol. J.W. Muth III, USMC, LtCol. J.A. Bass, USMC, LtCol. Ed Miller, USMC (Ret.), and LtCol. Gary E. Colpas, USMC (Ret.) are five of the best officers I have ever served with.

Col. K.A. Conry, USMC, my battalion commander in the Gulf War, is the type of officer all officers should strive to be like.

Capt. Bryan P. McCoy, USMC, is the best company commander in the Corps. If all Marines had his skill, intellect, and attitude, we would be the most dangerous armed force in existence.

SgtMaj. Wayne Smith, USMC (Ret.), showed me early on that if you just tell it like you see it, no matter whom you are telling it to, you will have few problems. He was right, as usual.

SgtMaj. Melvin "Mad Dog" Turner, USMC, is the calmest, most rational sergeant major I have ever encountered and served us well in the Gulf. Few could have done better.

SgtMaj. J.H. Lewis III, USMC, is as professional a Marine as there is. When he says it, you know it's a fact.

Master CPO Tom Keith, U.S. Navy SEALs (Ret.), continues to be a fighter the likes of which few men will ever equal.

My buddy, 1st Sgt. Rick Pelow, USMC, honored me with this book's foreword.

My mother and father somehow managed to keep me out of jail and more or less on the straight and narrow.

My wife, Susan, and daughter, Britta, are still with me. Sometimes I have no idea why.

Preface

This book is, as far as I know, the first and only one of its kind—a readable, informative, complete breakdown, analysis, and anecdotal description of Marine Corps special operations. Though original insofar as a concept goes, it was written with the aid of seemingly countless doctrinal military manuals produced by the Department of Defense, such as the Marine Corps' Operational Handbook 6-1 (*Ground Combat Operations*); various Fleet Marine Force Manuals (FMFMs); the insight and warfighting philosophies of officers and staff noncommissioned officers including Gen. Al Gray, USMC (Ret.), LtGen. William Keys, USMC (Ret.), LtGen. Robert Johnston, USMC, Col. Kevin A. Conry, USMC, LtCol. J.W. Muth III, USMC, LtCol. J.A. Bass, USMC, Capt. Bryan McCoy, USMC, SgtMaj. James Lewis III, USMC, Master CPO Tom Keith, U.S. Navy SEALs (Ret.); and my own experiences. Official military publications tend to be dry and very rigid, with few if any personal experiences woven into the fabric of the concepts and doctrine therein. This is the reason why, when Paladin Press' editorial director, Jon Ford, asked me to write this book, I agreed.

As you absorb the material between its covers, you will see that it is not only useful for military personnel but for anyone with an interest in or a need to know how the Marine Corps' special operations forces operate in this violent world we live in. It in no way is meant to replace doctrinal publications already in use but rather to supplement and complement them and to serve as a warfighting reference under one cover. I hope that my interpretations of the many concepts discussed herein, along with the anecdotes and historical references and examples, will serve to enliven what tends to become stale, impersonal dogma when bound in the text of the traditional military manual.

So grab your rifle and pack, and let's get under way.

Foreword

n 10 November 1775, the Second Continental Congress, in session in Philadelphia, resolved that two battalions of American Marines "be enlisted and commissioned to serve for and during the present war between Great Britain and the colonies." The United States Marine Corps was born. Since that autumn day so long ago, the Marines have served with distinction "in every clime and place," to borrow from "The Marines' Hymn," and are now frequently referred to as America's 9-1-1 force in readiness. But what makes the Corps, and especially its special operations forces, so unique?

The strength of the Marine Corps lies not in its arsenal of proven effective weaponry, nor in its future advanced amphibious assault vehicle (which will be capable of attaining speeds up to 25 knots in the water), or in the bizarre tilt-rotor MV-22 Osprey aircraft meant to replace the decrepit CH-46 Sea Knight helicopter. It lies in its young men and women who understand that being a Marine is about much more than learning a skill. They know that being a Marine is about courage, honor, tradition, and commitment. It's about duty before self and doing what needs to be done regardless of the consequences. Marines also know that whether they drive a truck, push papers, fix radios, or predict the weather, their first duty is that of a warfighter, an attitude that is demonstrated to every young Marine not slated for regular service in the infantry after graduating from recruit training—the infamous Marine boot camp—by his or her attending Marine Combat Training at the School of Infantry, of which the Corps has two. This course trains noninfantry Marines in the art of war on an entry-level basis and prepares them for future duties that might very well involve warfighting no matter what their regular job is in the Marines. Each Marine understands that it is this attitude that makes the Marine Corps so unique and successful.

This one-of-a-kind book is about warfighting from the Corps' special operations point of view. The author, a Recon Marine with 19 years of service and extensive time operating in the special operations arena, explains in terms understandable to not only the Marine or other military man but also to the layman interested in finding out just what makes the Corps' "spec ops" tick, and he includes frank discussions of the fundamentals of the offense and defense as well as the principles of war. He discusses maneuver warfare—the Corps' warfighting doctrine—and interlaces it with recent historical examples, many of which he was involved in. The author puts you inside the decision-making process that every Marine goes through when in combat and reinforces the fact that expeditionary warfare is the Marine Corps' most important mission.

Throughout its history, the Marine Corps has performed special operations in defense of American lives and interests. Marines have executed amphibious raids, boarded hostile ships and oil platforms manned by Islamic terrorists, rescued civilians from violence and natural disasters, reinforced embassies, and chased various criminal elements ranging from narcoterrorists in South and Central America to mail bandits in the United States. Gen. A.M. Gray, the twenty-ninth Commandant of the Marine Corps, who is rightly credited with the reinvigoration of the Marines and a renewed stress on warfighting skills being maintained at all levels, gave Marine Expeditionary Units the label SOC, indicating that they were "special operations capable." The title is new, the mission is old. Marines have been performing special ops for years.

A special operation is a tactical action that often results in strategic significance. A strategic objective of the United States is its ultimate goal or aim and is decided by the president, Congress, and ultimately the American people. Oftentimes this objective must be secured at a moment's notice by military might, and the Corps' MEU (SOC) units forward-deployed at sea represent a highly mobile and versatile force available for use on that objective. The MEU (SOC) force's combat power is multiplied by Marine and Navy air power and can be used in conjunction with class acts such as Army Rangers, Special Forces, and the skillful 82nd Airborne Division out of Ft. Bragg. Frequently the MEU (SOC) itself is enough to convince a potential or proven aggressor of American resolve.

Traditionally, Marines have been at the forefront of every American war. They fought in the Revolution and the War of 1812 against the British. It was the Marines who raised the flag over the Mexican fortress of Chapultepec during the Mexican War, and it was the Marines who captured seditionist John Brown at Harper's Ferry in 1859. They were the first U.S. troops to occupy Cuban soil, and they protected American interests during the Boxer Rebellion in China. The Corps drove terror into the hearts of German soldiers during the vicious battle of Belleau Wood in France during The Great War. After a series of violent mail robberies in the United States in the early 1920s, Presidents Warren Harding and Calvin Coolidge ordered Marines to guard the mail—not a single successful robbery took place against a Marine guard. "Uncommon valor was a common virtue" amongst Marines fighting in the Pacific during World War II. "I've been to the front, and there is not a finer fighting organization in the world," was said of Marines fighting in Korea by Gen. Douglas MacArthur. Fifteen years later, Marines would be the first American ground combat forces sent into Vietnam. From Lebanon in the 1950s to Grenada in 1983, from Quang Tri province, Vietnam, to Al Jaber in central Kuwait, the Marines have led the way in war and peace.

I wish a book like this had been available to me when I joined the Marine Corps 16 years ago; it would have saved me countless hours of reading and deciphering information from applicable field and technical manuals, and I could have used it as a ready reference in the instructor billets I have held. It would have made me a smarter Marine and a smarter warfighter, and a smarter Marine is a better Marine.

The author has had an unusual career to this point, and he has some truly unique qualifications to write this book. He joined the Corps back in the mid-1970s after a stint at the University of Maine and signed up for the infantry. Less than two years later he had already been promoted to the rank of sergeant—no mean feat—and was promoted to staff sergeant with just over five years as a Marine. He made "gunny" the first time he was ever considered. His nearly two decades of world-wide service have seen him hand-picked for some unheard of assignments, including his being one of the first Marines assigned to the Navy Survival School in Maine and the first Marine to ever become qualified as an Advanced SERE instructor. While serving at the fabled school, he worked as the staff noncommissioned officer in charge of the school's field force (which teaches the application of survival and evasion techniques) and as a "hard cell" interrogator in the Resistance Training Laboratory. He was also the primary environment instructor for the sea and seacoast branch at the school's Tropical Environment Survival Training Course in the West Indies, and he ran the Advanced Evasion Course as well.

Prior to his assignment as a SERE instructor, Bob Newman was an instructor at the Corps' Landing Force Training Command, Pacific, and has served not only in various infantry billets ranging from 81mm mortar section leader and forward observer to weapons platoon sergeant and company gunnery sergeant, but has served as a recon team leader and reconnaissance company training NCO and ops chief. During the Gulf War he served with one of the Corps' most decorated combat units, the Magnificent Bastards of Second Battalion, Fourth Marines. He is currently a tactics instructor and squad advisor at the Staff Noncommissioned Officer Academy's Advanced Course at Camp Lejeune and is the author of numerous books and thousands of magazine articles and newspaper columns on outdoor skills, with credits in such publications as *Soldier of Fortune*, *American Survival Guide*, *Practical Survival* (where he was a contributing editor), and all the major national hunting and fishing magazines. He is a contributing editor for *Infantry Theory* magazine as well. These achievements make him the most published author in the Corps, an unexpected accomplishment for an enlisted man.

Bob has put into plain English the warfighting capabilities of the Marine Corps, and in doing so he teaches the reader in a lively and practical manner how to wage war in the realm of Marine Corps special operations. It's a must read for every rank, and it should be added to the Commandant's Reading List and placed in every military exchange's bookstore.

Long live the United States, and success to her Marines.

1st Sgt. Rick Pelow, USMC

Glossary of Acronyms

AAV—amphibious assault vehicle ("amtrac")
ACE—air combat element
AO—area of operation
BLT—Battalion Landing Team
CAAT—combined antiarmor team
CATF—Commander, Amphibious Task Force
CMC—Commandant of the Marine Corps
CO—commanding officer
COC—combat operations center
CONUS—continental United States
CQB—close-quarters battle
CRRC—combat rigid raiding craft
ECC—evacuation control center

FAST—Fleet Anti-Terrorist Security Team
FCE—forward control element
FEBA—forward edge of the battle area
FMFM—Fleet Marine Force Manual
FOME—focus of the main effort
FSSG—Force Service Support Group
GCE—ground combat element
HIC—high-intensity conflict
HRT—hostage rescue team
ISOPREP—Isolated Personnel Report form
LAAW—light antiarmor weapon
LAV—light armored vehicle
LCAC—landing craft, air cushioned
LIC—low-intensity conflict
LOD—line of departure
LST—Landing Ship Tank
MAGTF—Marine Air-Ground Task Force
MARG—Marine Amphibious Ready Group
MAU—Marine Amphibious Unit
MEF—Marine Expeditionary Force
MEU—Marine Expeditionary Unit
MIC—mid-intensity conflict
MOPP—Mission Oriented Protective Posture
MOS—military occupational specialty
MOUT—military operations on urban terrain
MSG—Marine Security Guard
NCO—noncommissioned officer
NEO—noncombatant evacuation operation
OP—observation post
PME—professional military education
RAC—riverine assault craft
RRC—rigid raiding craft
SAW—squad automatic weapon
SERE—survival-evasion-resistance-escape
SMAW—shoulder-fired, multipurpose assault weapon
SOC—special operations capable

SOTG—Special Operations Training Group
SPIE—Special Patrol Insertion-Extraction
SPMAGTF—Special Purpose Marine Air-Ground Task Force
SRIG—Surveillance, Reconnasissance, and Intelligence Group
TRAP—tactical recovery of aircraft and personnel
UAV—unmanned aerial vehicle
USA—United States Army
USMC—United States Marine Corps
XO—executive officer

Introduction

"It is strictly forbidden to delay local counterattacks while permission of the next higher headquarters is requested."
From an *Oberste Heersleitung* circular, 1916

hen the Soviet Union collapsed in late 1991-early 1992, setting adrift its many satellites in eastern Europe and Asia, the United States Marine Corps' elite special operations community, along with its likenesses in the Army (Rangers, Special Forces) and Navy (SEALs), began to contemplate what suddenly appeared to be an uncertain future. For decades, Marine Force Reconnaissance (Force Recon) and Division Reconnaissance units, as well as the primary warfighting entities they served (Marine Air-Ground Task Forces or MAGTFs, Marine Expedi-

tionary Forces or MEFs, Marine Expeditionary Units or MEUs, and Marine divisions), had been training to fight somewhat protracted engagements with Soviet Bloc forces and their seemingly endless array of Third World henchmen such as those found on Grenada in 1983. In addition to this primary focus, the Corps had been training its Force Recon Marines in the science of counterterrorism, affording them superior training with some of the world's top counterterror units and providing them with some of the finest weapons and equipment available for use by Force Recon Hostage Rescue Teams (HRTs). Now it looked as if all this preparation was for naught.

But as events around the globe began to unfold at an alarming pace, it became quite clear that a substantial number of countries that had been under Soviet influence intended to cause problems of their own, and that there were many other nations and factions with violent agendas out there that would have to be dealt with by Marine special operations forces. These ranged from warlords in the long-suffering African nation of Somalia and the descendants of former slaves in Liberia to Saddam Hussein's forces in Kuwait and the New People's Army in the Philippines. Our long awaited "peace dividend" had abruptly lowered its interest rates.

But there were other problems as well. With the downfall of the Soviet Union and America's worsening economic conditions made almost crippling by a budget deficit all but beyond estimation, the United States armed forces became an immediate target for cost-cutting measures advanced by Democrats and Republicans both. Starting in the late 1980s, the Army began slashing dozens of divisions from its roles, the Navy mothballed hundreds of ships, and the Air Force cut numerous fighter squadrons as a result of the now infamous "bottom-up review."

The Marine Corps Commandant, Gen. Al Gray, was a warfighting visionary who devoted his four years as the Corps' top general to restoring its combat power and unusual prowess at inflicting mayhem upon selected opponents (which some Marines believe was neglected under his predecessor, Gen. P.X. Kelley). General Gray had clearly made some enemies in Congress with his straightforward, gruff demeanor and no-nonsense attitude. When told by Congress to cut his forces from about 186,000 or so down to 159,100, he simply said no, he wouldn't do it. His reasoning was that to put the Corps at that figure wouldn't allow it to handle all the missions it was tasked with, and that it would certainly cost lives on the battlefield. Congress gritted its teeth and awaited his retirement, which came to pass in 1991 after the Gulf War had gone down in history (with an astonishing performance by Marine forces as well as hard-fighting Army units—especially extremely aggressive Special Forces outfits and armor units—and a clearly technologically superior Air Force and Navy). At that time, General Gray was relieved by Gen. Carl E. Mundy, Jr., who successfully argued that the figure General Gray recoiled at—159,100—was clearly untenable. After a great deal of wrangling in Washington, it was decided that the Corps would reduce its ranks to a "bare bones" number of 174,000. The Corps considered this a win, restructured to make the numbers work in combat, and carried on.

Now Congress and the president were faced with a sticky wicket. Here we have a Corps of Marines with just barely enough manpower to do the job and which is suffering from some serious equipment problems, one of the most grievous of which is its medium lift helicopter, the CH-46 Sea Knight. This old workhorse's day had come and gone many years earlier, and the Marines were now faced with the problem of replacing it. Futurists wanted the MV-22 Osprey, a peculiar mixture of helicopter and fixed-wing technology that was fast and powerful but at the same time was extraordinarily expensive and put together with concepts that could, and did, prove deadly to those inside it after a terrible crash into the Potomac River in the early 1990s. But more staid Marines felt that another genuine helicopter with medium lift capabilities and sufficient speed would fit the bill for far less money. (As of this writing it appears that the Osprey proponents have won . . . for now.)

Another problem arose with the decommissioning of many of the amphibious fleets' assault ships, especially Landing Ship Tanks (LSTs), which have the unique ability to sail right up to the beach and discharge men and equipment via an extendable causeway. These were never replaced, resulting in MEUs at sea having to berth their

Marines in the much larger multipurpose amphibious ships, effectively breaking the cardinal rule of never massing your men in a defensive posture in one spot unless it is absolutely necessary to reduce the chances of them all being lost with one well-aimed antiship missile, mine, or torpedo. However, the Navy brass believed then, and does now, that it can defend against such strikes with other ships and aircraft and its advanced defensive technology.

A third problem, this one more subtle, was morale. The manpower drawdown was raising hell with promotions, a fact that didn't sit very well at all with the Marines. To help ease their concerns, the Corps instituted the "up or out" policy, which states that any Marine staff noncommissioned officer below the rank of sergeant major (staff sergeant through master sergeant and first sergeant) who failed selection to promotion twice in a row within his primary military occupational specialty (MOS) and who had fewer than 18 years of service would be denied reenlistment at the end of that tour. This made competition all the more keen, and those who didn't measure up were, and still are, told to leave, resulting in faster promotions and a more professional staff NCO force. A similar policy is extended to officers below the rank of major.

Finally, one of the Corps greatest challenges, also caused by the drawdown, was the increased operational tempo. This meant that Marines would be required to deploy more often, which can adversely affect individual readiness insofar as family stability is concerned. To help alleviate this glitch, the Corps established programs to help prepare families left behind for the rigors of deployment.

The Corps has yet to field the Osprey (or any other replacement for the Sea Knight), and deployments around the globe continue without any serious threat so far from antiship ordnance. In the last few years, Marine special operations forces have successfully undertaken such operations as Sharp Edge, Battalion Landing Team 2/4's classic noncombatant evacuation operation in Liberia in 1990; Eastern Exit, the rescue of American citizens from Mogadishu via a daring long-distance helicopter raid in 1991; Restore Hope, the temporary reestablishing of what passed for order in Somalia during the famine of the early 1990s; Uphold Democracy, America's action to rid Haiti of Raoul Cedras; and, of course, both Desert Shield and Desert Storm. For the immediate future, it appears that the Marine Corps will continue to plan for and conduct its many global missions, most of which will be carried out by its MEUs afloat from the shores of South America and Africa to the Caribbean, Europe, the Far East, Middle East, and everywhere else it seems.

This book is designed to give you a clear understanding of just how the Marine Corps is set up to handle its various tasks, how it trains to accomplish them, and what might be expected of it in the future. In addition, some special insight will be shed upon how the Corps got to where it is today in the special operations community, with a close look at how combat leadership techniques have kept the Corps at the cutting edge. You'll also learn how the Marine infantry battalion is now capable of dealing directly with many special operations tasks as part of the Marine Expeditionary Unit and how the Marines' quasi-mythical Recon and Force Recon units train for and fight both on the modern battlefield and in the shadows of the terrorist's world.

Historical examples of missions gone wrong, with detailed looks at operations like the deadly *Mayaquez* incident in 1975, the Corps' disastrous foray into Beirut in the early 1980s, and even the seldom discussed Makin Island raid during World War II (which didn't really fail but didn't go as planned either) will demonstrate how the Corps tries to learn from its mistakes so as not to repeat them. We'll also examine how Marines and other special operations forces can complement one another, such as on the Caribbean island of Grenada in 1983, when Army Rangers and Navy SEALs ran into trouble and ended up asking the Marines for a hand. But that isn't always the case, for we will see how the Rangers and SEALs can and do return the favor, demonstrating that cooperation between the services and especially between these groups of remarkable men can be a positive thing, despite the friendly bantering. (Today, Army Rangers train on Navy special ops submarines, while Marines gain hostage rescue experience by training with the SEALs and undergo some of the most demanding training available anywhere at the U.S. Army's Ranger School.)

An uncertain future requires a certain force, and the various

MAGTF configurations afloat, forward-deployed, and positioned in a state of constant readiness in CONUS (the continental United States) allow the president a clear measure of flexibility in dealing with assorted threats to American citizens and interests abroad. This is precisely the catalyst behind the training and combat power for America's 9-1-1 readiness force.

CHAPTER 1

The Nature of the Beast

"Marines prefer to kill . . ."

Allan R. Millett
Semper Fidelis: The History of the United States Marine Corps

24 April 1980. North Arabian Sea, aboard USS Nimitz.

usk has fallen on the great gray ships of the Navy task force, slowly making way in the warm waters south of ancient Persia. Aboard the massive flattop named in honor of World War II hero Adm. Chester Nimitz, the hulking dark forms of eight RH-53D helicopters squat on the gently rising and falling flight deck, the deafening roar from their whipping rotor blades drowning out all sounds. Scurrying around the huge choppers are assorted sailors dressed in working uniforms of different colors, designating flight deck, fuel, crash and rescue, and other personnel, but the dim light cloaks the bright colors. The helos are piloted and crewed by Marines.

Steaming south of the carrier, the USS *Okinawa*, an amphibious assault ship loaded with Marines of the 31st Marine Amphibious Unit (MAU) out of the Marine base at Kaneohe Bay, Hawaii, quietly cuts the slate gray waves. Inside the weary ship is a platoon of Marine reconnaissance specialists drawing up contingency plans to board and take control of the Soviet eavesdropping vessel that has been tailing the MAU since its journey across the Pacific three months earlier. The Marines fear that the Soviet spy ship will get wind of any rescue attempt being launched from the Navy task force and warn its contacts in Tehran.

The ship turns into the wind, the pitch of the choppers' roar changes slightly, and the birds lift off from the carrier and turn toward the unseen shore. Also flying in the night sky are six C-130 Hercules aircraft that have just lifted off from the tiny island of Masirah in the Persian Gulf, three designed to refuel the choppers at their first refueling stop in the Dasht-e-Kavir (a dry salt lake bed southeast of Tehran), the other three ferrying the 120-man commando team (equipped with silenced automatic weapons and pistols) and an additional smaller force that's to be used as perimeter security, the road-watch team. (Also "on call" are at least one AC-130 Specter gunship to provide covering fire, if needed, for the assault force, as well as Navy fighter-bombers.) As the big transports make their way across the desert, the commandos continually go over the details of the mission and check and recheck their weapons and equipment.

Already secretly inside the target country, now known as Iran, are four Army Special Forces operatives under the command of Maj. Dick Meadows, a long-time Special Forces soldier who led the prisoner rescue force of the Son Tay raid in North Vietnam in 1970. They are there to assist in the transporting of the commandos via half a dozen Mercedes 2 1/2-ton trucks to the U.S. Embassy and Iranian Foreign Ministry. Soon the team will arrive at its first stop, a windswept and barren place code-named Watchband in the heart of Islam: Desert One.

You know the rest of the story—one of the massive helicopters of

Operation Eagle Claw impacted a C-130 on the ground, resulting in a tremendous explosion that killed the crews of both aircraft (five Air Force personnel and three Marines) and stunning the commandos who intended to rescue the 53 Americans being held hostage in Tehran at the direction of the Ayatollah Ruholla Khomeini and carried out by the Revolutionary Guard. As a result, the hostages would remain just that until the swearing in of Ronald Reagan as president, at which time the revolutionary government in Tehran immediately released them, fearing—almost assuredly so—swift and massive military action by the United States.

This tragic incident led the Pentagon to reexamine its special operations capabilities, with particular emphasis on the concept of joint service operations and the special command and control considerations that had proven so devastating during the doomed Iranian hostage rescue attempt. Interestingly, rather than scrap further plans for future joint service special operations, the military elected to vigorously pursue corrective action, believing that they would be the norm in the decades to come. They were right.

SOOTHSAYER

After the terrorist faction known as Black September (a clique of the deadly Palestine Liberation Organization led by future Nobel Peace Prize winner Yassir Arafat) murdered members of the Israeli contingent to the Winter Olympics in Munich in 1972, military forces around the world began to take notice of this hardly new but nevertheless shocking form of unconventional warfare. The war in Vietnam was winding down, with a peace treaty of sorts to be signed in a year or so, and military practitioners began looking ahead to see what the future held in store for them. A few enlightened individuals believed that terrorism would be used more and more frequently in the world theater, and some were of the opinion that Israel and selected European countries wouldn't be the only victims of this especially heinous form of warfare; America was expected to be on the target list as well. Given this philosophy, a handful of Marines began planning for the worst. One of these men was 1st Lt. J.W. Muth III, a former enlisted man with extensive experience in unconventional warfare as a Reconnaissance Marine in Vietnam.

In the late 1970s, Muth (now a captain with an admirable reputation for being a forward-thinking maverick) took command of one of the Corps' reconnaissance companies, "A" Company, Third Reconnaissance Battalion, which was a part of the First Marine Brigade encamped at Kaneohe Bay. The company's primary mission at the time was to gather data on enemy units by covertly inserting four- to six-man recon teams into enemy territory via a variety of means, ranging from parachute to scuba, with the latter often being launched from a submerged submarine. Captain Muth expanded the company's mission to include training in hostage rescue techniques (taught to the Recon Marines at the FBI Academy in Quantico, Virginia) and close-quarters battle (CQB), as well as clandestine ship-boarding techniques that may be needed in support of a hostage rescue. (The latter were practiced in the waters off the naval base at Pearl Harbor.)

Tribal terrorists move toward their next massacre prior to the Marines' invasion of Monrovia, Liberia, in 1990. USMC photo.

At this time, the company was loosely referred to as a RAT company, for Reconnaissance Anti-Terrorist, and its new missions became known as "stingray" missions. The concepts, training, and combat techniques developed during these early years were to later be known as direct action (DA), or simply as black missions. Missions involving hostage rescue and similar situations were delegated to the Corps' Force Reconnaissance companies in North Carolina, California, and on the island of Okinawa.

Both the Army and Navy were also breaking ground in the special ops field at this time, with the Army creating Delta Force and the Navy retooling its famous Underwater Demolition Team (UDT)/SEAL teams, which would eventually lead to the creation of the Navy's top counterterrorist/hostage rescue force, SEAL Team Six, out of the Naval Amphibious Base at Little Creek, Virginia. This situation—the Marines, Army, and Navy all maintaining special operations forces—led to a great deal of competition between the services

Reconnaissance Marines on patrol. USMC photo.

and was partially responsible for the deeply flawed decision-making process used to mount the Iranian hostage rescue mission. (The Secretary of the Army was under pressure from his generals to ensure the mission was given to the Army and the Army alone insofar as the actual members of the rescue team went, but infighting in the Pentagon overwhelmed the Secretary of the Defense. Not wanting to alienate any one branch of the military, he advised the president, Jimmy Carter, to agree to a joint-service mission involving all four branches of the military, with the rescue team commandos consisting of the Army's Delta Force commanded by Col. Charles "Chargin' Charlie" Beckwith. Unfortunately, no joint-service mission such as this had ever been attempted by the United States military. This unsettling fact was ignored by the president, who ended up personally controlling the mission from the White House, a fact that would only serve to add to the command and control and training problems experienced by the force.)

ADAPTIVE FORCE PACKAGING: A WORSENING WORLD

Beginning with the landing of the 32nd Marine Amphibious Unit in Beirut on 25 August 1982 (with the mission of acting as a buffer between the Palestine Liberation Organization, which was trapped in Beirut, and the Israeli Defense Forces so the PLO could redeploy to Tunisia) to when the Marines pulled out for the final time in 1984, it became increasingly clear that the world was becoming an ugly place. Besides the trouble in Lebanon, communist insurgencies were creating headaches in Central America, South America, the Caribbean, and elsewhere. Terrorism in Europe from the 1970s (which was one of the primary reasons the go-ahead was given for the creation of Delta Force during that turbulent decade) had carried on well into the 1980s, and insurrections such as the New People's Army in the Philippines (then home of the Subic Naval Station and Clark Air Force Base) continued to concern the government of the United States.

Soon it became clear that special operations forces like Delta Force and SEAL Team Six were numerically insufficient when it came to handling the ever-increasing threats to American interests around

Special operations Marines storm ashore. USMC photo.

the globe. To add to the angst, there were more than a few ranking, special-operations-hating Pentagon officials who were extremely displeased with the performance of Delta Force and with the Navy's new Red Cell SEAL unit created and led by a very aggressive SEAL commander by the name of Richard Marcinko, whose members drew the hatred of some high-ranking Navy brass by demonstrating that many naval installations were grossly susceptible to terrorist attacks. The answer to these problems lay in the development of the MEU (SOC) forces, which now roam the seas as forward-deployed expeditionary forces in readiness, capable of handling many of the problems or "small wars" that crop up with annoying regularity.

Today's MEU (SOC) forces are task-organized to conduct a variety of missions across the lower and middle tiers of the spectrum of conflict. These range from typical show-of-force operations and mobile training teams provided to developing nations to noncombatant evacuation operations (NEOs), tactical recovery of aircraft and personnel (TRAP) operations (one of the most likely missions for the

Marine special ops forces routinely train in Norway, among other scenic locales. USMC photo.

MEU [SOC] currently operating in the Mediterranean), in extremis hostage rescue missions performed by either the Force Recon or SEAL detachment operating with the MEU (SOC), and a host of others.

To better understand precisely how the MEU (SOC) operates, we must first look at how it approaches modern warfare through the principles of war.

CHAPTER 2

The Principles of War

"Man does not enter battle to fight, but for victory. He does everything he can to avoid the first and obtain the second."

Ardant du Picq
Battle Studies

 lthough styles and techniques of warfare have changed dramatically over the centuries, the nine principles of war have not changed. These fundamentals are for understanding the battlefield and how the decision-making processes are always affected by events as they unfold before the commander's eyes and ears. The principles, as understood and interpreted by those fighting the war, provide guidance insofar as how one event can shape another.

SURPRISE

The crew of the Iraqi battle tank in the photo, destroyed by Task Force Ripper south of Al Jahrah, failed to understand the principle of surprise and paid for this mistake with their lives. Marine combat forces have long stressed the importance of surprise as a tool to be used against an enemy and even use Gen. Waldemar Erfurth's (Nazi Germany, World War II) book *Surprise in War* as a primer for training in this topic. As Erfurth said, "The mere existence of new implements of war does not solve all military problems." This concept forces the Marines to never rely on superior weaponry alone.

An important consideration when you intend to use surprise, as seen by Marines, is that to be effective you need not remain completely undetected until the moment you strike. The key is to strike so that the enemy isn't fully prepared to deal with your assault at a certain

An Iraqi tank lies in death, the victim of a Marine attack. Photo by the author.

time and place. For instance, they may know full well that you are there, but they may underestimate your true combat power at a critical time and place, namely a decisive gap that can be exploited to shatter their defensive capabilities. Through the use of unexpected tactics, seemingly indecisive terrain features, thorough reconnaissance, speed, a variety of deceptive maneuvers, well-planned and executed night operations, sound security procedures, and the employment of forces, both numerically and by training (i.e., riverine, counterterrorist, cliff assault, etc.), where they aren't expected, surprise can be achieved.

UNITY OF COMMAND

The Marines learned the hard way about the importance of unity of command with a very costly, albeit successful, mission in May 1975: the *Mayaguez* rescue near the Cambodian island of Koh Tang, where

LCACs roar over the surface after being launched from an amphibious assault ship. USMC photo.

Marines retook the American merchant cargo ship *Mayaguez* and forced the release of its crew to the USS *Wilson*. (The ship, belonging to the Sealand Service Corporation and under the command of Capt. Charles T. Miller, was boarded in the vicinity of the Wai Islands by Cambodian communist forces.) Due to a total disregard of the principle of unity of command, about 40 percent of the initial assault wave was lost or wounded, and a second attack was permitted to go on even after the crew of the *Mayaguez* had been repatriated.

This operation was one of those singled out for discussion when the planning for Operation Desert Storm went into effect. The Marines did not want a repeat of the disaster at Koh Tang, where no single commander had genuine command and control of all the forces in the operation. Desert Storm, the Marines knew, would be a harsh test of unity of command, but as history now tells us, the lessons learned at Koh Tang did pay off in the sands of Kuwait and Iraq some 15 years later.

SECURITY

Never has the Corps been delivered so graphic a demonstration of the importance of security than on the morning of 23 October 1983. Battalion Landing Team (BLT) 1/8, the ground combat element (GCE) of the 24th Marine Amphibious Unit, was occupying a piece of flat ground at the Beirut International Airport. This was not the terrain the Marines wanted. The first MAU commander to land in Beirut in that decade, Col. James Mead, had informed the Reagan White House through the Joint Chiefs of Staff (JCS) that he needed the high ground surrounding the airport, not the low ground, and that the low ground was a killing field which was defenseless in the face of artillery, mortar, and automatic weapons fire from the hills and 3,000-foot mountains to the east. The Reagan administration completely ignored Colonel Mead's plea and ordered him to occupy what would soon become a deadly piece of terrain.

The 24th MAU relieved the 22nd MAU at the airport on May 30, 1983. The 22nd MAU had already received a clear demonstration of what to expect from the Islamic terrorists operating at will in Beirut on 18 April, when a truck bomb demolished the U.S. Embassy, killing 17 Americans, including a host of CIA officials who were meeting there. Despite this event and a car bomb attack on a Marine convoy on 18 October, sufficient antiterrorist measures were never ordered by the commander of the 24th MAU, Col. Timothy J. Geraghty, who apparently never asked to see the report on the findings of the attack on the embassy in April. So restrictive were the MAU's rules of engagement that sentries were not permitted to have loaded weapons, and any Marine fired upon had to first receive permission from a commissioned officer to return fire.

These facts led to a shockingly easy and murderously effective terrorist attack on the BLT headquarters at 6:22 on the morning of 23 October. A lone terrorist driving a flatbed truck packed with what FBI demolitions experts believe was approximately 12,000 pounds of explosives surrounded by perhaps dozens of butane gas canisters drove the vehicle directly into the building and detonated his bomb, leveling the building instantly, which came down upon the 300 or so

A Marine guards American citizens prior to evacuation during a NEO. USMC photo.

Marines and sailors sleeping inside. Two-hundred forty-one men died.

It was clear to everyone in Beirut and the watching world that the vehicle bomb was the weapon of choice of Islamic terrorists in Beirut, and it was just as clear why: it worked. Nevertheless, this was ignored by the MAU commander and the White House. Amazingly, even basic principles of the defense, such as keeping your forces disbursed until massing for the attack, were ignored. Why else would 300 Marines be billeted in what amounted to one huge, easily accessed target?

OBJECTIVE

Objectives must be realistic in terms of feasibility, i.e., do you have the combat power to take that objective, is it a worthy objective insofar as its contribution to the desired end result, and do all subordinate units understand what needs to be done and why (commander's intent). Examples of good objectives in Marine Corps history include the taking

A night vision camera captures a Marine fast-roping from a Huey. USMC photo.

of Iwo Jima and Belleau Wood, while poor examples include Beirut in the 1980s. Critical in the selection of an objective is the understanding by all unit leaders of their higher command's goals. Without this understanding, a commander cannot effectively select objectives that support the proverbial big picture. This was a classic failure at Koh Tang, when the second assault force was still sent into combat even after the crew of the *Mayaguez* was released. The mission had already been accomplished, yet many Marines were killed or wounded in that second wave.

MANEUVER

One of the first clear examples of maneuver warfare as Marines know it today came during World War I in France. After learning how heinously deadly German machine gun and artillery fire could be to troops that didn't use crafty tactics, the Marines employed the combined-arms concept to support maneuvers performed by units smaller than the

Grunts hit the deck after being inserted via CH-46 Sea Knight choppers. USMC photo.

norm. Massed Marine assaults conducted on open ground had been brutally ineffective, and the stubborn Germans at Belleau Wood were resisting all such attacks. The Marines adapted by breaking down units into more maneuverable size and using artillery and their Chauchat automatic rifles and Hotchkiss machine guns in a combined-arms effect that put the Germans in a dilemma. This was accomplished by hitting the trenches with arty and then cutting down the Germans with machine guns as they fled. Charging Marine squads added to the mayhem.

Through maneuver warfare tactics supported with the combined-arms effect, Marines are usually able to defeat numerically superior forces set in deliberate defensive positions. The ability to maneuver effectively is especially important in many types of special operations, right down to close-quarters battle, room- and building-clearing techniques, and in extremis hostage rescues.

MASS

Marine special operations forces are seldom in a numerically superior position. How then can they use the principle of mass to achieve an end? The answer lies in time and place.

The prudent use of mass can greatly increase à force's combat power if applied at a time and place that is truly decisive. Such a time and place means that the enemy's ability and/or will to fight is crushed, therefore ending the battle successfully. Gen. Vo Nguyen Giap believed that his use of mass at the Marine fire base in Khe Sanh during the Tet Offensive of 1968 would be sufficient to drive out the Marines, but he failed to fully appreciate the devastating firepower of artillery and air strikes supporting the stubborn leathernecks. He did not select the correct time to assault the base, as his attack came toward the end of the monsoon season. When the clouds lifted, his troops were left fatally vulnerable to close air support and the prying eyes of artillery and mortar forward observers.

As an example of how mass can work to one's advantage, look at the numbers involved in the Gulf War. During Operation Desert Shield, then MajGen. Robert Johnston paid a visit to Second Battalion, Fourth Marines at Camp 15 outside of the Saudi port city of

Cobra gunships support a Marine amphibious assault. USMC photo.

Al Jubayl. He gathered all his staff NCOs together to inform them of how he intended to use the principle of mass against the Iraqis, who were at that time (early January 1991) outnumbering us by a ratio of 3 to 1. He said that he intended to use air power to reduce the Iraqi forces and that the ground attack would not commence until that ratio was reversed and *we* were outnumbering the Iraqis by 3 to 1. He did just that, and we had no trouble whatsoever with the ground war when we selected the best possible sites and times to cross the line of departure and rush the miserable Iraqis.

SIMPLICITY

One of the most common missions performed by MEU (SOC) forces is the noncombatant evacuation operation (NEO). During January 1991, a MEU (SOC) force performed just such an operation when it rescued Americans from the U.S. Embassy in Mogadishu during Operation Eastern Exit. The plan seemed simple enough, with the Marines and SEALs flying aboard Marine CH-53E Super Stallion helicopters launched from their Marine Amphibious Ready Group (MARG), the helos refueling in mid-air. They would then land at or near the embassy, secure it, gather up the civilians, and leave. The plan got a little more complicated and hair-raising when aviation fuel sprayed the rescue party during refueling, soaking them. One spark would have blown the helo apart, but their luck held and the mission was a success.

In war, the simplest of things tend to go wrong with annoying regularity, thus the requirement for simplicity being the norm as often as possible. Simplicity means that orders and the commander's intent are more easily understood, which lend themselves well to the mission being accomplished.

OFFENSIVE

Perhaps one of the underlying reasons behind the Marine disaster in Beirut was the fact that Marines are an offensive force by nature and were not fully versed (and were certainly uncomfortable with, especially with the vulnerable terrain they were required to occupy) in defensive strategy. Preferring decisive action—which is seldom possible when in the defense—so that the Marines' will can be imposed on the enemy, special operations forces are taught that freedom of action is crucial to winning and that this is achieved through gaining and maintaining the initiative on the battlefield. This can only be done through the use of aggressive offensive tactics.

So aggressive were Marine (and Army) forces in the Gulf War that it became impossible to collect enemy prisoners of war as they surrendered. In countless cases, they were simply bypassed and ordered to march south until they were taken into custody by rear-echelon and follow-on forces behind the main attack.

ECONOMY OF FORCE

Supporting attacks and other actions not directly involved with the main attack must be manned with the minimum number of forces needed to conduct that portion of the operation. During Operation Desert Storm, Marines afloat in the Gulf represented just enough forces to get the Iraqis' attention, for the Iraqis feared an amphibious and heliborne assault from the water. Of course, those Marines never joined in the attack but did perform an important feign that drew Iraqi forces away from the point of the main attack.

Thorough planning aided by good intelligence allows Marine special operations forces to select the appropriate number of forces for supporting operations. Failure to determine the right number needed can easily result in the mission being more costly than necessary and perhaps even failing outright.

• • • • •

Amtracs are a combat multiplier. USMC photo.

The principles of war as interpreted by Marine special operations forces are of little use without a complete understanding of maneuver warfare fundamentals, of which there are 10. Let's head into Chapter 3 to get a look at them.

Maneuver Warfare Fundamentals

"The acts of a man are determined by his character."
U.S. Marine Corps *Small Wars Manual*

M aneuver warfare, at least insofar as recorded
history goes, dates back thousands of years and
can be seen as the decisive element in countless battles. The best maneuver warfare practitioners, history tells us, from before the birth of
Christ (the Theban defeat of the Spartans at
Leuctra in 371 B.C.) to the present (the valiant
defense of Grozny by irregular Chechen forces
pitted against overwhelming numbers and firepower belonging to the Russians in 1994-
1995), have always known that maneuver warfare must remain fluid and ever-changing to be
effective. Rare is the enemy who fails to adapt

A Saudi tank rumbles down the Sixth Ring Road toward Kuwait City in the last moments of the Gulf War. Photo by the author.

to his opponent's tactics, thus allowing that opponent to do the same thing to him again and again. If an enemy has the ability to adapt, he will. This necessitates constant change in maneuver tactics. Marines stress that it frequently is a fatal mistake to assume that the enemy does not have the ability to adapt to your tactics.

Marines use 10 fundamentals to apply the art and science of maneuver warfare, the first of which may surprise those not familiar with Marine thought processes.

PREVENT ANTICIPATION

Marine special operations forces regularly operate in situations where the enemy attempts to adapt quickly to the Marines' tactics and methodology, trying to anticipate what they will do next so that they (the enemy) can regain the initiative and dictate the terms of the bat-

LtCol. Kevin A. Conry, Commanding Officer of Second Battalion, Fourth Marines, was a master at preventing anticipation during the Gulf War. Photo by the author.

tlefield. This is prevented by avoiding hard-and-fast rules or "by the book" tactics, thus denying the enemy the opportunity to take the offensive by gaining and maintaining contact and developing the situation to their benefit. If intelligence believes that the enemy may be preparing its defense for a certain form of attack, Marines will try to make them believe that they had anticipated correctly by creating a ruse, such as feigning what was expected and then striking a decisive blow elsewhere where the enemy least expected it. Imagination and freedom of thought and action (through a decentralized philosophy of command) make this possible.

THE ACHILLES' HEEL

The key here is to determine what the enemy's vital weakness is—and there may be more than one—and mercilessly and relentlessly

An artillery forward observer with Fox Company 2/4 beside an M198 howitzer, a fine tool for finding the Iraqis' Achilles' heel. Photo by the author.

attack that gap or weak spot until the advantage is gained. From there you destroy his unit cohesiveness and his ability to react quickly enough to your actions. The Gulf War showed that, as expected, one of Iraq's critical weaknesses was command and control in that important decisions could not be made by local commanders; they had to receive guidance and permission from higher authority in Baghdad. Another major weakness was the Iraqis' stretched lines, where advance units were positioned in Kuwait far from supply points in Iraq itself. To these ends, the command and control apparatuses were laid to waste immediately, and bridges spanning waterways between logistical positions in Iraq and the frontline units were taken out. Vehicles that managed to make their way into Kuwait were continually running the risk of destruction at the hands of Marine Cobra gunship pilots, Army Apache gunship pilots, Air Force Thunderbolt II Warthog drivers, and other aviation assets patrolling Kuwait airspace.

LEAD FROM THE FRONT

The commander who does not personally assess the situation on the battlefield, who must constantly rely on reports from various sources instead of seeing for himself what is happening, is not in command of the situation. This basic truth requires commanders of Marine spec ops units to be well forward in the battle, shunning the compara-

Saddam Hussein failed to lead from the front and was crushed. Iraqi Ministry of Defense photo. Used without permission.

tive safety and comfort of rear areas. Selection of the commander's forward observation post (OP) is ultimately decided by the commander himself but is first considered through a thorough map study followed by reconnaissance of the site itself by a scout team or reconnaissance patrol. The commander hears the recommendations of the Marines who performed the reconnaissance and makes his decision, always having alternate plans and locations in mind and available.

The importance of the commander being forward located so that he can better command the battle cannot be understated. This is not to say, however, that the combat operations center (COC) is to be located with the commander at his OP. The OP should be located in the vicinity, but it should never be placed in so vulnerable a location as to allow the entire command staff, including the commander, to be killed or wounded with one artillery or mortar round. Communication links between the commander and the COC must be reliable so that information between the two is assured.

THINK AND ACT PROACTIVELY

By thinking and acting proactively, Marines are able to dictate the terms of the battlefield to the enemy, therefore developing the situation as they see fit. The key is to keep the enemy reacting to your advances, probes, attacks, and other offensive actions so that he never gains the upper hand and must continually fight in the defense. The force that operates at a higher tempo and uses fire and maneuver to keep the enemy off balance is much more likely to win, provided actions taken are directed at destroying the enemy's unit cohesiveness and at limiting or crushing his will to fight.

The war in the Pacific theater during World War II is a classic example of this, where Marines hopped from island to island at a rapid rate to gain a strategic advantage, while on a tactical level commanders tried to keep the enemy reacting to continual assaults.

EFFRONTERY WITH DECISIVENESS

Mere audacity isn't enough to win battles with any continuity.

A Marine sniper
understands
thinking and acting
proactively. Photo
by the author.

Audacious maneuvers require objectives that will prove to be decisive, and unwarranted acts of effrontery only serve to tell the enemy about your state of mind and tactical decision-making process.

War, especially within the realm of special operations, is filled with uncertainty, risk, and chance. But at the same time, opportunity may arise in such a fashion that the commander who acts first upon it,

Decisive action frequently results in morbid humor at the hands of a Marine with a can of spray paint. Photo by the author.

even when there is substantial risk involved, may very well win the day. The trick is to weigh risk against gain and make a decision quickly. Imaginative tactics employed with sheer gall when the enemy least expects them have won more battles than we will ever know.

SgtMaj. Melvin D. Turner, who served as the senior enlisted advisor to the commander of the 24th MEU (SOC) in Somalia during Operation Restore Hope, says that the Marines had a very simple policy when dealing with the various warlords' bandits and thugs: massive and rapid retaliation. It was simple: if a Marine was shot at, the entire area the enemy shooter fired from would be destroyed, while at the same time fastidiously avoiding injuring innocent civilians and abiding by the law of war. This policy rapidly gained the cooperation and respect of the enemy, and, according to the sergeant major, within a few days a Marine could walk down most any street in Somalia "bucknekked" and completely unarmed without fear of bodily harm.

EXPLOIT SUCCESS

The gambler knows that a single dollar won at blackjack can be parlayed into many more dollars in a very short period of time if he has command of the game. If you're hot, you're hot, as they say. This can be translated into warfighting parlance by exploiting the successes of subordinate units at a rapid tempo and with orders and plans that are flexible enough to adapt quickly to new situations. First used by the Germans in World War II and known as the "recon pull," Marines adopted this fundamental in Korea and later showed just how effective it is during the Gulf War. Like the domino effect, one event influences another. The most common mistake is not reacting quickly enough to fully exploit a nearby success, thus giving the enemy the chance to prevent any exploitation later planned.

The Cobra gunship is a superior means of exploiting success. Photo by the author.

DECENTRALIZATION OF COMMAND

This is clearly one of the Marine special operations unit's most valuable assets, and it is a fundamental first stressed at recruit training, where recruits are told of the fact that any Marine may find himself faced with having to make a decision in combat, regardless of his rank. Because of this belief, leadership principles and techniques are part of the everyday life of Marines, who must be prepared to both take command and make quick, correct decisions in times of tremendous stress and uncertainty. Critical to this ability is the commander's ability to make his intent clear—*this is what I want to achieve*, or *this is my objective*—while the actual subordinate unit tactics are left to be decided by junior officers, staff NCOs, NCOs, and in some cases non-NCOs (lance corporals, privates first class, and privates).

A great advantage to fighting this way is the special operations

Any Marine might find himself in command at any time. Photo by the author.

forces' ability to maintain the highest possible op tempo. The commander who insists on making tactical decisions for his subordinate units will never realize his command's true combat power.

A typical example of this was Second Battalion, Fourth Marines' taking of a portion of a migrant workers' camp in southern Kuwait known as the "ice cube tray" for its appearance from the air. Fox Company rolled up onto a slight rise in the terrain shortly after dark fell on the first night of the ground war in Operation Desert Storm and could see this massive installation spread out before them. Iraqi tanks and other armored vehicles were being engaged by combined anti-armor teams (CAATs) to the front of the company, freeing the assault amphibious vehicles (AAVs, or "amtracs") with the infantrymen inside to do the actual taking of the facility. When the company commander, Capt. Andrew Schlaepfer, saw the complex, he informed the battalion commander, LtCol. Kevin A. Conry, who told him to take it at his pleasure. No orders were given as to how he was to take it, only that he was to take it.

One of the AAVs with a 60mm mortar team and the weapons platoon sergeant (the author) stopped and fired an illumination mission that lit up the buildings and surrounding area, while the remainder of the company (which had recently performed the noncombatant evacuation operation known as Sharp Edge in Liberia) assaulted and captured the complex.

A corps of capable, aggressive staff NCOs makes the implementation of a decentralized philosophy of command realistic and practical for the Marines. All staff NCOs receive continuous professional military education (PME), including training in all aspects of warfighting regardless of each Marine's particular MOS. This is necessary because of the Corps' extremely high enlisted-to-officer ratio of 9 to 1, the highest such ratio in the U.S. armed forces by far.

THE "FOME"

A fundamental of the offense is concentration of combat power. To best bring to bear that combat power at a decisive time and place, the commander must decide which unit(s) he will make the focus of

Support must go heavily to the FOME. Photo by the author.

the main effort, or FOME. Once he selects which subordinate unit will be doing the dirty work, every available supporting asset is directed to that unit. This is a combat power multiplier that must never be overlooked or given less than its due.

As we know, risk, uncertainty, and chance are always present in varying degrees on the battlefield. At this point the commander must decide how he can use economy of force to his advantage by taking away some combat power from supporting units so that the FOME has sufficient power to do the job right the first time. This tends to put those units whose combat power has been temporarily reduced at risk, resulting in uncertainty. This is an example of how risk comes into play. A thorough and accurate assessment of the enemy situation will lessen this risk.

ABILITY AND WILL

It is crucial that Marine special operations forces not get wrapped around the proverbial axle in thinking that the taking or indirect control of key terrain is going to win the battle. Although there are historical instances of how the direct or indirect control of a certain piece of terrain did in fact bring the battle to a close, warfighters for centuries have known that terrain usually only hastens or aids the winning of the battle, as opposed to winning it outright.

Many Marine planners believed that the Marine taking of the port of Inchon and subsequent splitting of the North Korean forces across the peninsula would bring a quick end to the war. It did not. Intelligence failed to predict that the Red Chinese would come to the aid of their North Korean comrades when it became clear that they were in peril. This resulted in the war being exceedingly prolonged, not ending until the summer of 1953.

Use key terrain as an asset, but never believe it is going to be the single factor leading to the successful prosecution of that battle.

Marine special ops personnel must have both the ability and will to take the fight to the enemy. GySgt. R.L. Weaver, USMC, photo.

Instead, focus on whatever it takes to strike a genuinely decisive blow that hinders or altogether prevents the enemy (in a physical form) from fighting or destroys his will to fight.

COMBINATION PUNCHES

Champion boxers don't become so by developing and using a single punch exclusively. They know that they must have a variety of tricks up their sleeve if they want to win. This fundamental, when applied to warfighting, is called fire and maneuver.

Maneuver, even in its simplest and least risky form, must be supported by fire from either weapons organic to the maneuvering unit or in direct support of it (as when an artillery battery is put in direct support of an infantry unit, a measure championed by Napoleon), or preferably a combination of both. Critical to the success of the maneu-

The Harrier is an excellent means of delivering the combined-arms effect. USMC photo.

ver is how the supporting fire is used. For special operations units to achieve the most combat power during the maneuver, the combined-arms effect must be used.

By employing two types of weapons against a single enemy force, such as the Mk19 heavy machine gun (essentially a fully automatic, belt-fed grenade launcher) and M60 machine gun, the enemy can be placed in a predicament from which there is no escape. For example, Marines frequently engaged Iraqi troops who refused to come out of their trenches and surrender by walking high-explosive Mk19 rounds down one end of the trench to push the Iraqis out the other end, where they were cut down with by M60 machine guns and squad automatic weapons (SAWs).

• • • • •

Now that we are familiar with the principles of war and maneuver warfare fundamentals, we should examine the spectrum of conflict and how Marine special operations forces are specifically tailored to meet the innumerable threats existing within this realm.

CHAPTER 4

The Spectrum of Conflict

"In personal combat, it is often difficult to determine where defense ends and offense begins."

Col. Rex Applegate
Kill or Get Killed

T he Marine Corps and, as of late, its special operations forces (which were originally termed "raider units," first conceived during World War II in the Pacific and implemented with such units as Merritt Edson's First Raider Battalion) have normally been viewed as forces for use in the lower reaches of the spectrum of conflict (this is especially true today, when the Corps is at a precariously low strength of about 174,000). In this arena, military actions are likely to take the form of all manner of contingency operations and various rescue missions (NEOs, TRAPs), as well as more offensive actions such as counterterrorist ops (where Force Recon "direct action" teams would engage terrorists in what would hopefully be a very brief encounter, ending in the deaths of all the terrorists and the liberation of any hostages). However, the normal operations of the Corps' MEU (SOC) forces usually find them simply marking time near some hot spot such as Bosnia, Somalia, Liberia, Grenada, or even Sicily (where the 24th MEU [SOC] attempted to

THE SPECTRUM OF CONFLICT

Stability Ops (Civil/Military Ops)	Limited Objective Military Ops	Conventional Combat Military Ops	General War
(A) Presence	(A) Peacetime Contingencies	(A) Amphibious/ Airborne Ops	(A) Amphibious/ Airborne Ops
(B) Humanitarian Assistance	(B) Counter-terrorism Ops	(B) Subsequent Ops Ashore/Inland	(B) Subsequent Ops Ashore/Inland
(C) Mobile Training Team Assistance	(C) Counter-narcotics Ops	(C) Continental & Maritime Campaigns	(C) Continental & Maritime Campaigns
(D) Security Ops	(D) Counter-insurgency Ops		
(E) Peacekeeping Ops			
(F) Antinarcotics Ops			
(G) Demonstration Ops			
(H) Antiterrorist Ops			

plug Mt. Etna, a volcano threatening several villages and towns, with huge concrete blocks dropped from its CH-53E Super Stallion helicopters in 1992).

Given this, Marine spec ops forces must have an understanding of just what types of operations across the spectrum of conflict they can be expected to perform, with emphasis on low-intensity conflicts.

A BRIEF HISTORICAL OVERVIEW

When one examines how the Corps has been employed over the centuries, it becomes clear as to why it has become the force of choice for low-intensity conflicts. For instance, it is noted in the Corps' *Small Wars Manual* (first printed in 1940 and released again in 1987) that the Marines made over 180 landings between the years of 1800 and 1934 in 37 countries. The only conflict during that time that cannot be considered as falling into the realm of low-intensity conflict (or at the most mid-intensity conflict—the Spanish-American War) was World War I. World War II was a radical change for the Corps, and five years later this costly lesson was followed by the Korean War. Although Korea doesn't qualify as a high-intensity conflict, it easily falls into the upper mid-intensity conflict range.

The Corps intervened in Lebanon in 1958 and the Dominican Republic in 1965 and also landed in South Vietnam in 1965. It has been incorrectly stated that America's Vietnam War was a low-intensity conflict, and the basis of this erroneous argument is the fact that it did not physically spread outside a very small theater, that being North and South Vietnam, Cambodia, and Laos. The problem here is that one cannot differentiate between low- and mid-intensity conflict on the sole basis of ground covered. Other factors that must be taken into account are the length of the war (eight years in this case), the amount and types of ordnance expended, casualty figures, and the level of manpower on each side. This makes it clear that the Vietnam War was a mid-intensity conflict.

After Operations Frequent Wind and Eagle Pull in 1975, the Corps was fairly quiet for seven years except for the occasional involvement with such operations as Eagle Claw in Iran. Then the Marines landed once again in Beirut in 1982, departing in 1984. They made the landings on Grenada in 1983, conducted counterguerrilla ops against Iranian maritime guerrillas in the Persian Gulf in the late 1980s, and went into Panama during Operation Just Cause in December of 1989. The next year saw Operation Sharp Edge in Liberia, where more than 2,400 noncombatants were safely evacuated from Monrovia by special operations forces belonging to the 24th MEU (SOC); Operation Eastern Exit in Somalia, where 241 noncombatants were evacuated by like forces; and of course the Gulf War's Operation Desert Shield. In 1991 they were heavily involved in Operation Desert Storm.

The 1980s and 1990s also saw Marines involved in various aspects of counternarcotics operations in Central and South America as part of the Drug Enforcement Agency's (DEA) Operation Snow Cap and others. Operation Restore Hope in Somalia and Operation

Marines of Fox 2/4 are promoted by Lt. Col. Kevin A. Conry during the Gulf War.
Photo by the author.

Distant Runner in Rwanda brought the Marines back to Africa once again, and in 1994 the Marines returned to Haiti as part of Operation Uphold Democracy. Marine Fleet Anti-Terrorist Security Teams (FAST) provided security for the United States Liaison Office in Mogadishu, Somalia, and in late February and early March of 1995, Marines again stormed ashore in Somalia to withdraw the United Nations peacekeeping forces there for what is hoped to be the final time in Operation United Shield. (This complex operation was the first time the Marines were equiped with special nonlethal crowd-control weapons such as wooden and rubber bullets, grenades that when detonated produce a terrible stinging effect like that of a swarm of bees, and a device that sprays a very sticky goo onto rioters, which immobilizes them almost instantly.)

With a history like this, it is small wonder that the Corps' MEU special ops forces, the brainchild of former Commandant Gen. Al Gray, continue to prepare for future low-intensity conflicts. With their unique ability to project a sea-based forward presence on short notice and react to myriad threats in both the low- and mid-intensity conflict categories, they are expected to continue to have a high operational tempo well into the twenty-first century.

MAKING THE TARGET LIST

Prior to deploying and while afloat, MEU (SOC) staffs perform regional studies guided by intelligence reports that indicate which countries in their AO are potential threats. To this end, the Marines have developed an equation of sorts that helps them determine which countries are susceptible to low-intensity conflicts that could involve U.S. forces. There are three prominent factors they consider, any one of which could produce a conflict. However, unless all three factors are present, it has been shown that a conflict is unlikely to develop.

A Vulnerable Population
The following list of elements might be present in varying degrees:
1) an agrarian society marked by primitive agricultural means
2) an underdeveloped educational system

3) minimal raw materials available for export
4) an underdeveloped industrial base
5) substantial population growth outpacing economic growth
6) low percentage of citizens with industrial or technical skills
7) capital assets generally controlled by foreign nations
8) governmental corruption and ineptitude
9) absence of investment capital

Efficient Insurgency Leadership

An organized and dedicated insurgency leadership hierarchy can make a tremendous difference when gaining broad-based support from the populace.

Lack of Governmental Control

Governments that have sufficient control over the populace are less likely than those that do not to suffer from an insurgency.

In addition to the above, studies are directed at the political reasons behind the problem. In my low-intensity conflict class at the Staff Noncommissioned Officer Academy Advanced Course at Camp Lejeune, North Carolina, I stress to students the importance of understanding why a conflict is occurring in a certain nation or region and why Marines are used at times to bring the conflict to an end, hopefully. Examples I give are both positive and negative. Positive include Grenada, Haiti (both joint-service ops with the Army), Liberia, Cuba, and Somalia; negative include Lebanon (the second time around).

Grenada was easy to understand in that a communist overthrow of the democratic government on that tiny Caribbean island had been set up through middlemen supported by the Soviet Union and Cuba. The Marines were used to rescue the Americans on the island and remove the communists, who were building a military runway long enough to launch long-range bombers. Liberia was a little trickier, with several factions of guerrillas all trying to kill each other and gain control of the country. Americans were there and needed to be rescued. Haiti had become a dictatorship after the overthrow of its first democratically elected leader, and "boat people" were fleeing the island and coming to American shores en masse, an untenable situation. The exodus of Cuban refugees in boats to American soil was likewise unacceptable, and the refuge camp at Guantanamo had to be opened and manned by Marines. And the most treacherous conflict, in Somalia, involved widespread famine and warlords causing hate and discontent among the masses. Marines broke the famine and prevented the warlords from running amok with the supplies coming in to the port at Mogadishu.

But these admittedly simple explanations are insufficient when it comes to planning and conducting an operation designed to bring the conflict to an end. The root problems of each are unlikely to be assailable by Marines alone, a fact which almost always requires the Department of State and other agencies to become directly involved in the mission. Marine special ops forces can handle the combat facets of the operation, but they cannot stay in-country indefinitely

A SMAW rocket is fired at a bunker. Photo by the author.

without the cause being worked on by political entities. The history of the Marines is rife with actions taken in certain countries again and again because the problems were never solved on a diplomatic level. And Marines, although adaptable, generally do not make good diplomats unless specifically trained to do just that, such as the Marine Security Guard (MSG) detachments at every American embassy and consulate.

Although the term is still widely used, "peacekeeping" operations is a misnomer. No Marine special operations force has ever been used to keep the peace anywhere: they are used to crush those forces deemed dangerous in nations already experiencing some sort of turmoil through the aggressive acts of another armed force. A form of MAGTF may establish *order* once ashore, but a genuine, lasting peace is highly unlikely. This is only attainable through diplomatic means backed up by the threat of force. We have seen what happens when you put an offensively oriented "peacekeeping" force into a fallacious situation such as Beirut in the early 1980s, with no fathomable mission but to occupy a static defensive position between a melange of warring factions bent on one another's complete destruction.

Today's wide-ranging Marine special operations are backed up by intense diplomatic efforts which, if effective, allow the Marines to spend as little time on the operation as possible. Before Marines are sent in, their mission is very carefully scrutinized in Washington to try to ensure that they are truly needed.

● ● ● ● ●

That is a look at low-intensity conflict as it applies to the MEU (SOC) or other form of MAGTF. Next on the horizon is a study of the offense.

CHAPTER 5

On Offense

"It's the way that I move, the things that I do."
Elton John
"The Bitch Is Back"

he Marine Corps' warfighting philosophy is built around the offensive fundamental of fire and maneuver, which is also a maneuver-warfare fundamental. Through the use of fire and maneuver, Marines direct their efforts to accomplish one or a combination of seven objectives:

1) the destruction of enemy forces and equipment

2) the acquisition of combat information or intelligence

3) the occupation or indirect control (through indirect fire) of key terrain features

4) the disruption and deprivation of enemy logistical capabilities and resource acquisition

5) the restriction or total denial of enemy movement from a certain location

6) the diversion or deception of enemy forces

7) the hindrance of enemy operations while they are in the defense

These objectives are achieved through an understanding of the principles of war and the judicious application of the 15 offensive fundamentals.

OFFENSIVE FUNDAMENTALS

All of the greatest tacticians in history—from Patton, Rommel, and Puller to Hannibal, Khan, Sherman, and Hooker—had a solid grasp of the importance of offensive fundamentals. The commander

One means of maintaining contact with the enemy is through sniping. Here, Capt. David Close fires an M40A1 sniper rifle. Photo by the author.

who understands these basics and finds himself facing one who does not is almost a sure winner.

Find Them and Keep Them Found

Before any attack can be initiated, you must first gain and maintain contact in some fashion with the enemy. From this basic premise all else follows. This can be done through a variety of means, ranging from sensor devices clandestinely planted by Reconnaissance Marines that detect enemy movements to the ultimate form of contact—hand-to-hand combat.

During the Gulf War, Marine reconnaissance teams were deep inside Iraqi-held Kuwait days before the ground war kicked off, gathering information that was crucial for target selection and tactics. When ground reconnaissance wasn't available, the Marines used unmanned aerial vehicles (UAVs) to keep an eye on the enemy.

Reconnaissance Marines use various insertion methods to help develop the situation.

Photo by the author.

Get to Know Him

While maintaining contact with the enemy, you must constantly develop the situation by ascertaining his troop strength, disposition (how he is set up and what passive and active actions he is taking in the defense), and composition (what types of troops he has, his equipment, etc.). This is done through reconnaissance measures and the analysis of intelligence.

During the Vietnam War, MACV-SOG kept deep reconnaissance teams along the Ho Chi Minh Trail in both North and South Vietnam and Cambodia to better gauge what the enemy was up to. These stealthy teams were highly effective in learning what types of enemy forces were moving along that warren of paths, trails, and roads beneath the jungle canopy, and many communists were killed by spoiling attacks conducted from both the ground and air before they ever reached their objectives in South Vietnam.

Pick Your Target and Hit It Hard at the Worst Possible Moment for the Enemy

Where, when, and with what you conduct your attack is of critical importance in all offensive maneuvers. The trick is to deliver a decisive blow at a point and time that the enemy cannot effectively defend against, and this is made easier by your developing the situation well. Find his most vulnerable and costly weakness, then attack it mercilessly until he submits.

A decisive blow is usually sudden and shocking and destroys the enemy's resolve. The Marines were on the receiving end of such a fundamental on the morning of 23 October 1983, when an Islamic terrorist destroyed the BLT headquarters building at the Beirut International Airport. This single act crushed America's resolve, and the Marines left.

Take Advantage of Gaps

A gap in the enemy's combat power need not be physical—it can be more intangible in nature, such as inexperienced troops or low individual and unit morale. By developing the situation and constantly evaluating intelligence reports, you can determine his vulnerabilities and work to exploit them.

Iraqi vehicles lie destroyed in the United Agricultural Research Facility in a Kuwait City suburb. Photo by the author.

Gaps may be on dry land or along waterways. Here a Marine riverine assault craft maneuvers up a river. Photo by the author.

The Vietcong and North Vietnamese Army were masters at finding and exploiting gaps in perimeters. A "sapper" would crawl toward the Marines' barbed-wire-covered perimeter in the darkness with a satchel charge and then toss it into the barrier, blowing a hole in the wire. Immediately, a line of enemy troops would rush through this gap and destroy whatever they could with grenades and additional sachel charges.

Jump Him

Surprising the enemy is probably the oldest form of maneuver warfare. It has survived all these millennia because it works. A numerically inferior force, through surprise, can achieve success under many different situations. However, disaster is likely for the maneuvering unit that loses the element of surprise and does not have an alternate plan.

One means of achieving surprise is through the airborne insertion of special ops Marines. GySgt. R.L. Weaver, USMC, photo.

Navy SEALs turned the tables on the enemy in South Vietnam by adopting the tactics of the communists—namely, deadly ambushes. As the SEALs became better and better at hitting enemy patrols in the jungle and along the river systems, the Vietcong would put more and more emphasis on trying to kill the SEALs, but the Navy commandos usually beat them to the punch. The more audacious the ambush the better, the SEALs believed in many cases.

The Quick and the Dead

Rare is the successful offensive maneuver that isn't performed with calculated rapidity. In this instance we refer to both operational tempo and the actual rate of physical movement of forces. Estimates, plans, and actions must all be performed at a higher rate of speed than the enemy. He who is fastest dictates the terms of the battlefield.

The best recent example of this is the Marine incursion into

Marine Hummers equipped with TOW missiles are a proven means of rapidly closing with the enemy. Photo by the author.

Kuwait from 24 February to 28 February 1991 and the Army's infiltration into Iraq during the same time period. The ground forces were moving so quickly over each objective that the enemy never really had much of a chance to react to the remarkable tempo set from the first moments of the war. Aggressive men armed with superior weaponry can be difficult to keep pace with, as the Iraqis found out.

Get Moving and Keep Moving

Your momentum in this instance isn't your rate of movement but the expansion of your own combat power brought about through the application of other fundamentals. Anything you do that increases your combat power and helps to keep the enemy off balance is momentum.

Continuing with the Gulf War scenario, once the Marines crossed through the berm and mine fields and "got up to speed," they

Armored vehicles such as this amtrac allow Marines to maintain their momentum. Photo by the author.

knew that it was important to keep rolling forward. Like the prize fighter who staggers his opponent with a quick shot to the face, they continued to advance and strike, advance and strike, until the enemy either surrendered or died.

Beat Him to the Punch

"Do unto him *before* he does unto you" is the golden rule of the

The crew of this Iraqi tank did not survive the Marines' punch. Photo by the author.

offense. By taking the battle to the enemy, you force him to fight on your terms and make him react to your actions. This concept is a combat power multiplier.

On 6 October 1973, thousands of Syrian tanks roared into Israel across the Golan Heights just as Egyptian forces struck a thunderous blow across the Bar Lev Line. This was one of the greatest military surprises in history, and the Israelis were taken aback. In the middle of the afternoon, two of Israel's most feared enemies had attacked in unison, and Israel was nearly decapitated in the opening throws of the Yom Kippur War. Had the Syrians and Egyptians been able to maintain their momentum after this incredible surprise, things may very well have turned out differently.

Unmitigated Audacity

Maneuvers that shock, unnerve, and catch the enemy unaware demonstrate the bold and aggressive attitude projected by Marines. The idea is to perform maneuvers that the enemy decided you wouldn't or couldn't do because they were too outlandish and risky. An enemy who thinks like this creates gaps for you.

In 1950, after the North Korean People's Army charged into South Korea, there was but a single gap left exposed on the right flank of the enemy advance—Inchon. This harbor has tremendous tides and represented a difficult solution to an even tougher problem, but it was determined that if the Marines could somehow land quickly at Inchon, they could break the enemy's assault on Pusan. The communists didn't suspect a thing, believing that such a maneuver would be impossible to pull off. But the plan worked like a charm, and the communists were stunned.

Shoot, Move, and Communicate

This is fire and maneuver. The combined-arms effect (putting the enemy in a dilemma with multiple weapons systems) reinforces this concept so that the enemy cannot counter your maneuvers effectively.

Although the war in the Pacific during World War II was generally one of attrition, Marines employed fire and maneuver heavily in taking back the Pacific islands from the Japanese. Squad and fire

The Special Patrol Insertion-Extraction (SPIE) rig is one audacious method used by special ops Marines. Photo by the author.

teams used automatic weapons and flamethrowers to suppress enemy fire while a Marine or two rushed the enemy's position with demolitions or grenades. Such tactics were highly effective although obviously extremely dangerous.

Recon Marines are specialists at shooting, moving, and communicating. The parachute is just one means used by covert recon teams to feed information to and thus facilitate the fire and maneuver of ground forces. GySgt. R.L. Weaver, USMC, photo.

Kick Him When He's Down

You should have no "problem" in piling it on when successes are realized. Keep in mind that your objective is to win with the fewest possible friendly casualties. Each enemy allowed to escape is an enemy who will be sighting in on you the following day.

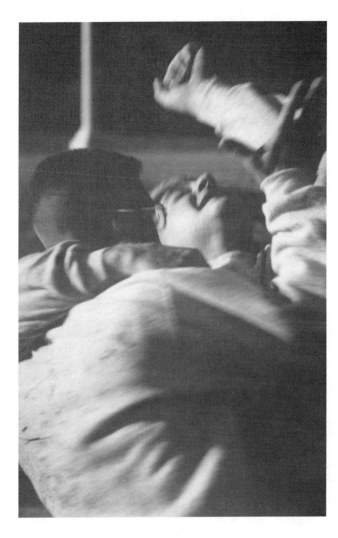

Hand-to-hand combat is taught to all Marines regardless of their likelihood of having to deal with the enemy in such a manner. Photo by the author.

Unless they are in the act of surrendering or have already been captured, all available enemy forces should be wiped out. This was the policy in the Gulf War, and it worked very well. Marines were surprisingly understanding and lenient when Iraqis tried to surrender, but when they did not, the Marines were merciless. Consider the Highway to Hell between Kuwait City and Basra, where Marine air and Army armor combined to massacre retreating Iraqis.

Cover Your Back

One breach of security is all the enemy may need to destroy your combat power and gain the upper hand, thus putting you on the defensive. Security is a constant concern yet is one of the easiest things to overlook, especially when all appears to be going well.

Marine patrols in Vietnam learned costly lessons in security while on the move. Dispersion is critical while en route to the objective, and security efforts to the front, flanks, and rear must all be focused equally. Marines learned that, in many instances, the place the enemy was most likely to attack from was the one that appeared least likely.

The Iraqis manning this tank did not cover their back. Photo by the author.

Plan B might include a cavalry charge, as this Marine in Kuwait appears to be contemplating. Photo by the author.

Plan A and Plan B

Given the number of battles fought since man commenced organized warfare, one might think that he would have become more adept at offensive tactics by now. This is not the case, primarily due to the chaotic nature of the battlefield and the many uncertainties that lie there. No one can truly plan for every eventuality, but you must develop the situation well enough so that most potential problems are anticipated and planned for.

When the Argentinians invaded the Falkland Islands, they had only one plan, a plan that didn't anticipate the resolve and combat power of the British government. This failure to plan for multiple scenarios resulted in the British romping the Argies, although the queen's

Terrain during the Gulf War was basically flat, with critical subtleties. Photo by the author.

men did suffer some horrifying setbacks such as the loss of the *Antelope, Atlantic Conveyor, Sheffield,* and other ships.

The Real Estate Market

Countless battles have been fought over terrain that both parties believed was key. Despite remarkable advances in weaponry, we have seen over the centuries that terrain still remains crucial in many battles. One need not actually occupy the terrain to gain an advantage; an advantage can be attained by simply denying it to the enemy through indirect control measures (mines, artillery fire, close air support, etc.).

When Army tanks and infantry fighting vehicles seized Mutlaa Ridge overlooking what was about to become the Highway to Hell during the Gulf War, the Iraqis stood no chance of survival. This was key terrain, and with Marine air raining death from above·

Marine reservists serving with Second Battalion, Fourth Marines in the Gulf War proved indispensable for their warfighting prowess. Photo by the author.

and Army armor obliterating the enemy from the flank, the results were inevitable.

The Stun Gun

Every effort must be made to neutralize the enemy's ability to counter your actions. One means of doing this is to use the combined-arms effect with whatever resources are available: artillery, close air support, mortars, heavy machine guns, naval gunfire, etc. Just as the "stun gun" is used by police to incapacitate a criminal, Marines must use whatever is at their disposal to prevent the enemy from reacting effectively to their maneuvers.

The .50-caliber machine gun on the Marines' amphibious assault vehicles was used to prevent the Iraqis from reacting effectively during bunker- and trench-clearing operations in the Gulf War. When the .50 machine gun was used in conjunction with the Mk-19 heavy (40mm) machine gun and other automatic weapons, the Iraqis found they had a difficult time maneuvering for anything but their survival, if that.

MANEUVERS

Because Marine special operations forces are not designed to fight protracted engagements over long periods of time with tens of thousands of troops, their tactics are designed to defeat the enemy quickly. To this end, Marines keep their tactics simple and brutal and use both these maxims to multiply their combat power. Which maneuver they select to accomplish a particular objective is determined by using a decision-making guide known as METT-TS-L, which allows the commander to make an accurate estimation of the situation. The elements of METT-TS-L are Mission, Enemy, Terrain and Weather, Troops and Fire Support Available, Time and Space Available, and Logistics.

Mission

Key to mission accomplishment are "commander's intent"—the mission—and orders that allow subordinate commanders to determine how they will get the job done. Always included in this section are plans for additional and alternate missions should the situation change during the battle.

Enemy

This is an estimate of the combat power of the opposing force, with attention being paid not only to his strengths, composition, and disposition, but his weaknesses. Every appreciable factor must be weighed when determining strong points and gaps, including terrain, training, morale, weaponry, logistical capabilities, routines, penchants, customs, and level of alertness.

Terrain and Weather

We will never know how many battles have been won or lost because of an inaccurate estimate of the importance of a certain terrain feature or weather system. Even terrain features and weather factors that appear to be minor can become critical in short order. Giap, despite his warfighting treatise *People's War, People's Army*, failed to grasp the criticality of the monsoon's lifting at Khe Sanh in 1968, and his forces were decimated by being exposed to accurate artillery fire and air strikes made all the more effective by Marines still in possession of the high ground.

Marines use the acronym KOCOA to assess terrain and weather.

K: key terrain
O: observation and fields of fire
C: cover and concealment
O: obstacles
A: avenues of approach

Due consideration of each of these factors must be paid in order to gain an accurate assessment of the terrain and weather.

Troops and Fire Support Available

The units selected to be the main attack, supporting attack, and reserve must be chosen carefully to match each mission. Of special interest here is the Marines' concept of the reserve. Unlike many other armed forces, they see the reserve as not being a force used primarily to step in when the main attack has failed but rather as a force used to exploit success. However, should the battle go bad, the reserve can be used to regain the initiative.

Thought must be given to how much and what type of fire support is available and how each type is going to be assigned, be it general, direct, or attached.

Time and Space Available

Confederate Maj. Gen. Nathan Bedford Forrest stressed the importance of his units arriving on the scene of the battle being "the first with the most." (Gen. Robert E. Lee considered Forrest to be the greatest tactician and strategist of the Civil War.) Forrest saw time as being critical. This precept still stands. Speed is everything in battle.

Space refers to maneuvering room. Consideration must be given to both imposed and natural boundaries, and each must always be considered a gap: imposed boundaries because the link between adjacent units is intrinsically weak, and natural because no terrain feature is truly impenetrable or otherwise invulnerable.

Logistics

Every Marine has logistical concerns: does he have enough ammunition for his rifle, grenades for his assault vest, gasoline for his vehicle, and water for his canteen? Minute errors in calculating what is needed at all levels can stop an attack in its tracks, literally, while too heavy a logistics load will impede speed and momentum.

That's METT-TS-L. Now, once the situation is understood, the commander must decide upon a course of action by selecting a form or forms of maneuver to be employed and used with the combined-arms effect to best achieve his objective.

Frontal Attack

This is the least desirable form of maneuver insofar as it intentionally strikes at the enemy's strongest point. However, it is used only under certain circumstances where it is decided that through speed and momentum the enemy can be quickly overrun or taken down

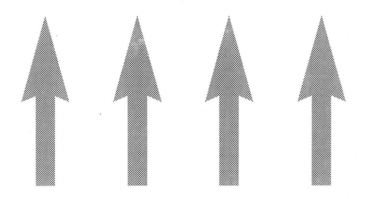

A frontal attack.

from behind as he attempts to break contact. A frontal attack can also be employed as a ruse designed to deceive the enemy about the real main attack about to strike elsewhere.

The frontal attack with a focused penetration is a maneuver that intends to break through enemy lines with a penetration at one point. We normally see three phases of the penetration—rupturing, widening, and seizing. The rupture is where the breaching force punches a hole through the lines at one narrow spot using whatever means are available, such as the M1A2 bangalore torpedo, M1E1 projected charge kit, or M58 line charge. The gap created is widened immediately to allow as many assault forces as possible through in the shortest time—a critical consideration given the murderous nature of such an operation—and then seizing the objective through close combat or whatever means are called for.

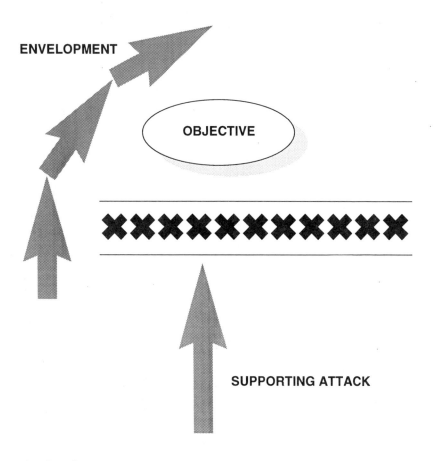

A single envelopment.

Single Envelopment

The single envelopment is much preferred over the frontal attack, as it seeks weak points (gaps) and is less risky. The main force maneuvers around (or over in the case of a heliborne assault) the heavily defended areas and attacks through gaps in the enemy's rear. This destroys unit cohesion, weakens command and control, and disrupts the enemy's logistics.

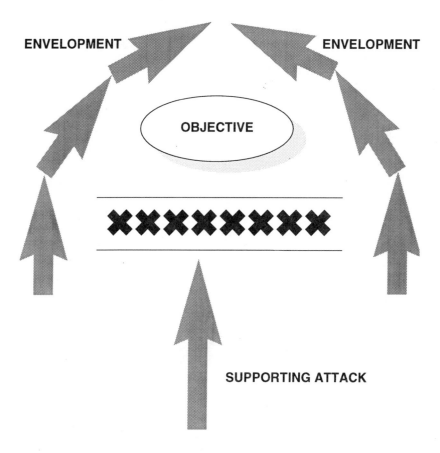

A double envelopment.

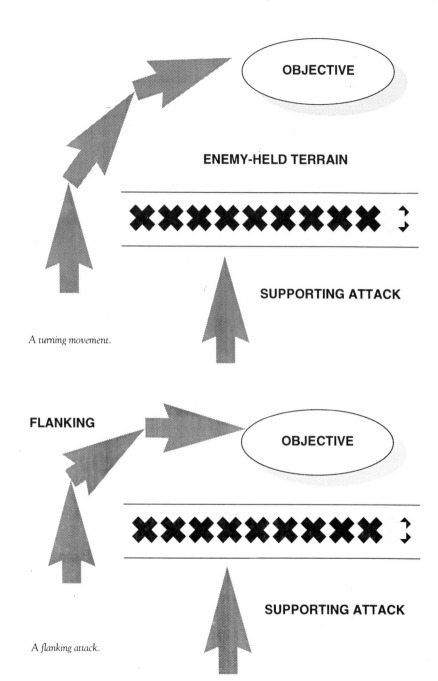

OBJECTIVE

ENEMY-HELD TERRAIN

SUPPORTING ATTACK

A turning movement.

FLANKING

OBJECTIVE

SUPPORTING ATTACK

A flanking attack.

Although not mandatory, a supporting attack elsewhere (such as along the enemy's front) to deceive him while the envelopment is underway is highly recommended. A strong reserve is also very important so that the success of the envelopment can be exploited to its fullest. It may be determined that a double envelopment would best suit the attacker's needs, but superior coordination and surprise are a must.

Turning Movement
Designed to force an enemy unit out of its position without ever engaging it directly, the turning movement is used as a deep disruption technique that cuts the enemy off entirely from support, which forces him to relinquish the terrain he is on because of his sudden vulnerability due to an absence of logistical and support assets or because he must now attack the force that has cut him off. This is an excellent maneuver when time allows and is often used by a numerically inferior force.

Flanking Attack
Done on a shallower axis than is an envelopment, the flanking attack uses surprise to assault the enemy's flank where he believes you will not do so due to some perceived obstacle. Because it is less risky, it is also less decisive in many cases. Remember, with great risk often comes great gain.

HEDGING YOUR BET

If at all possible, you must hedge your bet by using a supporting attack somewhere along the enemy's position in order to convince him of something you want him convinced of. For instance, a supporting attack (using as few troops as possible so that the main attack is allowed the principle of mass) could be used to draw the enemy's reserve into action early on and at a place away from the main attack, thus preventing an effective counterattack on the main force. His main body could be engaged by the supporting force in order to draw their attention away from the main attack trying to envelope him. It can also be used to bamboozle him into thinking that you are about to do something the enemy is prepared for and is hoping you would try, and also to concern the enemy about a potentially key terrain feature you appear to want to occupy.

The supporting attack can also suddenly be made the main attack if unexpected weakness is encountered there. Supporting arms (artillery, air, mortars) must be ready to support either force.

FINISH HIM OFF

In the offense, Marines use their reserve force for one primary purpose, and that is to exploit success. The reserve destroys any hope the enemy had of successfully defending his position, and this force must be prepared, like supporting arms, to support either the original main attack or the supporting attack that has unexpectedly hurt the enemy badly.

●　●　●　●　●

Those are the basics of offensive maneuvers. Next we will examine the six forms of offense as seen by Marines and then look at the various actions Marines engage in within those forms. As you might expect, despite this world of F-117A Stealth or Wobbly Goblin attack bombers and cruise missiles that fly through windows, the fight frequently comes down to the Marine on the ground with a rifle, a pocket full of grenades, and a bad attitude.

CHAPTER 6

Bread and Butter:
Offensive Operations

"The leadership and the command must have great initiative, resolve and daring."

General Vo Nguyen Giap
How We Won The War

ffensive operations are divided into six categories. By making a thorough and accurate estimate of the situation, the commander can best decide what he needs to do and where and when he needs to do it in order to strike that all-important decisive blow.

OPERATION CATEGORIES

1) deliberate (the most preferred, which uses a detailed reconnaissance plan and is used when time allows)
2) hasty (the opposite of deliberate;

used when you don't have time for a detailed reconnaissance plan)

3) reconnaissance in force (the use of a pretty-well-armed recon force to determine the enemy's combat power in a certain area)

4) movement to contact (just as it says—when an enemy force is engaged by simply moving forward until contact is made)

5) exploitation (such as the Coalition's relentless chasing and disruption of Iraqi forces in Iraq and Kuwait so that they were never given an opportunity to reestablish their defense or counterattack)

6) pursuit (taking exploitation one step further and killing or destroying every legitimate target)

OFFENSIVE ACTIONS

There are offensive actions involving actual violence or threatened violence through the potential for immediate conflict, and there are those that are more benign. It is important to note that simply because massive destruction or a decisive engagement is never intended or expected, such a scenario should never be discounted. Given this, thorough, careful planning is the norm from start to finish, and the maneuvering force must be prepared at all times to take up another mission should a decisive gap be discovered and immediate exploitation be required.

First, let's look at those that are violent or threaten to be so.

Raids

The first genuine raid conducted by Marine special ops forces was in August 1942 by companies A and B of the Second Raider Battalion, led by LtCol. Evans Carlson, where the Marines raided Makin Island in the Pacific from the submarines *Nautilus* and *Argonaut*. In a fascinating return to this concept, Army Rangers and U.S. Marine special operations forces began training for submarine-launched raids in 1994, using the *Kamehameha* out of Pearl Harbor as their platform.

The raid differs from all other actions by having a planned withdrawal. Raids are swift and ideally undetected until too late, and they are normally performed by a company or platoon. Means of entry

Raids are quick and dirty and always have a planned withdrawal. USMC photo.

include rigid raiding craft (RRC), combat rigid raiding craft (CRRC), riverine assault craft (RAC), helicopter, and foot. In rare cases, a force recon platoon might use parachutes. Surprise, speed, and high mobility are critical, and the objective may be anything from a diversion to the rescue of civilian hostages or American prisoners of war.

There are as many different reasons for conducting a raid as there are things that could go wrong. Destruction of structures and/or materiel, the capture of enemy personnel and equipment, the creation of a diversion as a supporting attack for the main attack being conducted elsewhere, collection of information, and use as a probing attack are only a handful of reasons raids are employed.

Noncombatant Evacuation Operations (NEOs)

NEOs are fairly routine for Marine special ops forces serving with a MEU (SOC), and they differ from a raid in two major ways: the level of planned violence is greatly reduced, and the NEO may very well

NEOs are one of the Corps' most frequent ops. USMC photo.

take much longer (months in some cases) and therefore involve the seizing and holding of quite a bit of terrain. Other differences are that frequently a greatly dispersed and irregular enemy is employed, and the withdrawal date and time can be somewhat vague.

NEOs are missions that routinely end up before the eyes of the world, with various media organizations present and recording what oftentimes seems to be every move the evacuating force makes. In the interest of appearing humane, Marine special ops forces recently evacuated the United Nations "peacekeepers" from Somalia and were equipped with more than their usual weaponry. This time they had rubber and wooden bullets, special grenades used for crowd control that are nonlethal but produce a nasty stinging effect, and even a sticky foam sprayed from a man-portable pack that clings to rioters and virtually immobilizes them. Of course, these weapons, which were first seen during the riots in Los Angeles in the summer of 1992, do nothing to encourage rioters to cease and desist. Rioters know that their actions will result only in inconvenience rather than death or dismemberment, and concern has been voiced about this.

Demonstrations

Marine amphibious forces in the Gulf War executed demonstrations along the Saudi coast as a show of force and ruse of sorts. They wanted the Iraqi forces in Kuwait to believe that an amphibious assault would be conducted once the ground war started, but this never happened. However, the Iraqi hierarchy was planning its defense of Kuwait City to include defending against an amphibious assault. True demonstrations do not intend to engage the enemy at any time, only to make him think or act a certain way because of an implied threat.

Demonstrations must be performed by a force large enough and seemingly powerful enough to convince the enemy that what

A demonstration of military power and resolve is sometimes sufficient to deter any action by a potential aggressor. USMC photo.

he is seeing is not a demonstration but an attack heading his way. Failure to convince the enemy of this will free him to look for the real attack elsewhere, possibly resulting in the discovery of that force prior to its assault.

Feints

It has been incorrectly stated that the Marines aboard amphibious ships in the Persian Gulf during the Gulf War conducted a feint in sailing closer and closer to Kuwait City as the ground war kicked off. This wasn't a true feint, for true feints seek a limited engagement. The amphibious task force never sought to engage the Iraqis, and never did, although they were fully prepared to do so if its mission had changed suddenly.

Supporting attacks frequently are feints, engaging the enemy at a certain place and time in order to draw his attention away from the

Artillery is a good method of supporting a feint to make it appear to be the main attack. USMC photo.

main attack elsewhere. They can be of any size, but economy of force must be considered so that the main effort has sufficient mass to conduct its attack.

Hard-Point Actions

Hard points are individual fortifications within a larger system of fortifications that are mutually supportive, treacherously positioned (no discernible gaps, thus requiring the dreaded frontal assault with a hoped-for penetration), and extremely difficult to assault

Fortified positions, such as this Iraqi bunker, must be hit hard and with great force and speed. Photo by the author.

successfully. The one predominant prerequisite for taking such a position is *overwhelming combat power.* Without this, the attacking force's demise is all but certain.

The use of combined arms, aggressive small-unit actions marked with a substantial degree of audacity, and a powerful and highly mobile reserve force ready to exploit any success during the battle are absolutely crucial.

Marine special ops forces spend long hours planning for such operations, given the propensity for high body counts on the attacker's side when planning and preparation are wanting. Marines fully expected to have to assault heavily fortified Iraqi positions in Kuwait, and their training in the Saudi desert prior to crossing the line of departure (LOD) was tightly focused on trench-, tunnel-, and bunker-clearing tactics. As it turned out, the frequency of these actions was not nearly as great as expected.

Siege Reliefs

Should a Marine raid or other action go bad and the force become trapped in some fashion with no means of breaking out without assistance, another Marine force may attempt to break that siege by attacking the enemy force that has the original force in a jam.

Command and control is especially important in such an action, and much thought must be given to the use of combined arms and the rearward passage of lines by the relieved force (i.e., when the relieving force attacks the enemy and takes some pressure off the pinned-down force, which then moves through the new force's lines and heads for a safe area). The relieving force must be fully prepared to conduct a running gunfight with pursuing enemy forces as they withdraw. The key lies in forcing the enemy to defend rather than attack by making multiple threats to his survival. Maneuvers should be constant and fluid during such an operation, with a high operational tempo that keeps the enemy reacting to the new force's actions.

Infiltrations

Used in support of the main attack, infiltrations are conducted using stealth and guile while avoiding contact with the enemy or any

The light armored vehicle is a good platform from which to conduct a running gunfight. USMC photo.

other form of detection. A study of the enemy's defensive perimeter is made, and a gap (or gaps if multiple breaches are required) is selected for use by the infiltration team. The infiltration team(s) must be clear as to what its exact mission is so that it can best support the main attack when it occurs. Therefore, it is important that an alternate plan be ready for initiation should the infiltration be discovered before the main attack force is in place and ready to strike.

Urban Actions

Offensive military operations on urban terrain (MOUT) present Marines with special problems. To this end, the Corps has constructed realistic "combat towns" at both Camp Lejeune in North Carolina and Camp Pendleton in Southern California, complete with sewer systems and other urban features, to help teach Marines how to fight in a city.

Urban ops run the full gamut for Marine forces, ranging from the NEO where not a shot is fired to vicious house-to-house tactics such as

Infiltrations conducted by partisans such as this Kuwaiti resistance fighter are frequently easier and more effective than those conducted by Marines, who may not look indigenous. Photo by the author.

Hue City during the 1968 Tet Offensive in Vietnam. During the latter, key terrain is seized that allows coverage of the penetration point. Once a foothold is established, the gap there is widened as quickly as possible so that follow-on forces can drive deeply into the city with the hopes of splitting the enemy's forces or otherwise causing hate and discontent by upsetting the enemy's plans and forcing him to react to you.

Pretense Actions

Also known as holding attacks (a term that is rather misleading),

This airfield represented an urban environment in many respects, and a tremendous fight occurred here between Marine and Iraqi forces. Photo by the author.

pretense actions are those actions undertaken in support of the main attack that serve to draw the enemy away from the main attack, much in the way a feint does. But pretense attacks have sufficient combat power to keep the enemy engaged for a protracted amount of time, where feints do not.

As a battle at OP 4 in northern Saudi Arabia on 29 January was developing, another major attack was developing at OP 6 of about the same gravity. The enemy attempted to divert the Marines' attention from these attacks by conducting probing attacks all along the front, which served as pretense actions apparently meant to hold adjacent units in place so that holes could be punched through the Marine defenses at OPs 4 and 6.

OTHER ACTIONS

Those actions not intentionally involving directed violence or

Marines use a sand table to plan an attack. Photo by the author.

which do not necessarily expect an encounter with an opposing force—but which still might become violent because of the uncertain nature of all battlefields—include the crossing of obstacles, passage of lines, linkups, and other such actions. Marines stress remaining prepared for any eventuality during these actions, as a crafty enemy will see them as potential gaps and want to exploit them.

The Gulf War saw Marines crossing a complex obstacle belt in the form of mine fields covered by Iraqi artillery, mortars, and tanks, which required exquisite coordination at all levels. At some breach points there were firefights, while others were pretty quiet. The same war found Marine units linking up so that gaps would be minimalized. At some of these connecting points, Iraqi units attacked, such as when Second Battalion, Fourth Marines linked up First Battalion, Eighth Marines in the area known as the "ice tray," while other linkups were uneventful.

• • • • •

Now that our understanding of the offense in general is workable, a look at some special operations themselves is in order.

CHAPTER 7

Selected Special Operations

"A military victory is worthless if it fails to be politically convincing."

Abraham Guillen
Urban Guerrilla Strategy

I t has been wrongly stated by unrealistic proponents of the Marine Corps that its force of 174,000 is capable of handling anything that comes this nation's way short of general war on a theater level or large airborne operations. This is a ludicrous claim and one that ignores the true nature of modern warfare on a planet where third world dictators such as Saddam Hussein or Hafez al-Assad of Syria have the ability to cause tremendous turmoil across a broad area. The Marines could not have defeated the Iraqi forces in Kuwait without the help of the Army, Air Force, and

Navy. It's that simple. And when it comes to some forms of special operations, such as supporting a growing democracy movement in an impoverished backwater nation, the best force out there is the Army Special Forces, or "Green Berets."

It boils down to this: the Marines are primarily meant for low-intensity conflicts that pop up quickly and need to be handled with dispatch by a forward-deployed force that has the ability to support itself for a few weeks without needing major logistical assistance from the American mainland. Such a force is the MEU (SOC). In the event of a little larger brawl, a Marine Air-Ground Task Force (MAGTF) as large as a Marine Expeditionary Force (MEF) can be deployed, which is self-sustainable for as long as 60 days. The nation also has the option of using a smaller, specially created Special Purpose Marine Air-Ground Task Force (SPMAGTF) such as those that followed the MEU (SOC) ashore in Liberia and Somalia.

MEU (SOC) forces are required to be able to perform an array of special operations, including special demolitions ops, noncombatant evacuation ops, in extremis hostage rescues/counterterrorism ops, security ops, tactical recovery of aircraft/personnel, amphibious and heliborne raids, counterintelligence ops, deception ops, and many others. They must be able to launch any contingency operation they are given within *six hours* of tasking. This is made feasible by rapid response planning.

SPECIAL DEMOLITION OPERATIONS

The Corps' demolitions expertise has come a long way in the last decade, particularly when viewed from a mine field-breaching standpoint and the use of high explosives to facilitate the rapid entry of an in extremis hostage rescue team into a room or structure. Marines involved in the latter (Force Recon Direct Action teams trained by the Special Operations Training Groups' Special Missions Branch) are the "duty experts" when it comes to CQB involving hostages, and the use of high explosives by these teams is commonplace. This requires a knowledge of demolitions that goes far beyond the scope of this book. However, we will examine the basics of demolitions from the viewpoint of normal operations of the MEU (SOC).

Definitions

High Explosive: Those explosives that convert from a solid to gaseous state at a rate no less than 3,280 feet per second (fps) and up to 27,888 fps.

Low Explosive: Those explosives that convert from a solid to gaseous state at a rate up to 1,300 fps.

Cratering Effect: The ability of an explosive (usually low) to remove destroyed material from a crater.

Shattering Effect: The ability of an explosive to destroy materials.

Relative Effectiveness Factor: The effectiveness of an explosive in cratering, cutting, or breaching in comparison to the same abilities of TNT.

Types of Explosives

Amatol: A mixture of TNT (trinitrotoluene) and ammonium nitrate found in outdated bangalore torpedoes. The mixture is kept in an airtight container to avoid accidental detonation (it is hygroscopic, i.e., readily absorbs moisture).

Ammonium Nitrate: An explosive with low sensitivity used frequently with composite explosives that are highly sensitive.

Black Powder: Still having its uses, black powder is found in some fuzes, detonators, and igniters and is a mixture of sulfur, charcoal, potassium, and sodium nitrate.

Composition A3: Consisting of 91 percent RDX and 9 percent wax for binding and desensitization, Comp A3 is found in some bangalores and in shaped charges.

Composition B: The primary force behind shaped charges, Comp B is made up of 60 percent RDX, 39 percent TNT, and 1 percent wax. One of the fastest-detonating explosives.

Composition B4: The latest bangalores contain Comp B4 (60 percent RDX, 39.5 percent TNT, and 0.5 percent calcium silicate), as do some shaped charges.

Composition C4: Generally known as C4, this is a favorite of special ops forces because of its moldability, versatility, and power. It contains 91 percent RDX and 9 percent benign plasticizers.

Cyclonite: Also called RDX, cyclonite is most often seen in use as a composite explosive and in certain blasting caps. Extremely powerful.

Military Dynamite: More stable than commercial dynamite because it does not contain any nitroglycerin at all, military dynamite is a mixture of 75 percent RDX, 15 percent TNT, and 10 percent plasticizers and desensitizers.

Nitroglycerin: Rarely if ever used due to its volatile nature. Its sensitivity, as portrayed in countless Hollywood movies, is basically true.

Pentaerythrite Tetranitrate (PETN): A very versatile and extremely powerful explosive used in various ways, such as in composites, detonating ("det") cords, booster charges, and blasting caps.

Pentolite: Boosters for shaped charges can be made with pentolite, a mix of half TNT and half PETN. Fast and powerful.

Tetryl: Less common now than a decade ago, tetryl has a variety of uses. It is not as powerful as its replacements (PETN and RDX) but is still useful when these are not available.

Trinitrotoluene (TNT): One of the most commonly used and effective explosives. Many uses, including booster charges, as a composite explosive, and as a bursting charge.

Doing the Job

Marine special operations forces may be required to use explosives for an array of problems ranging from cutting a bridge's steel truss superstructure and creating a crater for an antitank ditch to cutting trees in order to form an obstacle along a likely avenue of approach and knocking a door down behind which terrorists are holding hostages. This makes determining the type, explosive power, and placement of the charge(s) critical.

Eight factors are considered in getting the job done right the first time. Using too small a charge or using the wrong explosive or explosive mix may result in the mission having to be retried. Using too large a charge might result in friendly casualties or the damage or destruction of other objects that you don't want messed up. I once used far too big a cratering charge while operating in the Philippines as a reconnaissance team leader because I failed to take the permeable nature of the soggy ground into account. I wanted a crater about 5 feet deep and 10 or 12 feet wide and ended up with a gaping hole 15 feet deep and 30 feet across. The large rocks and boulders the blast sent skyward traveled for quite a distance and reached impressive heights before falling back to earth, destroying one village hut and scattering the natives like rats from a burning ship.

The eight factors for preparing for a demolition operation are:

1) *Composition*: What is the target constructed of, i.e., steel, concrete, reinforced concrete, wood, iron, etc., and how rugged is it?

2) *Dimensions*: What are the dimensions of the target, with special consideration given to weak points that can be exploited?

3) *Objective*: What effect do you want to have on the target? Partial or total destruction? Shifting and moving (pushing dirt and rocks aside)?

4) *Explosive*: What is the best available explosive for the job?

5) *Size and Shape*: How much of the selected explosive(s) is needed, and how will you configure the charge?

6) *Placement*: Where will the explosive(s) be placed and how will it be secured there?

7) *Initiation*: How can the charge best be initiated?

8) *Tamping/Stemming*: What must be done once the charge is set to tamp or stem it so that force is not lost or misdirected?

There are countless situations that could confront Marine special ops forces which might require special demolition operations. While conducting counterterrorist ops in the Persian Gulf against Iranian-backed terrorists operating from oil platforms, it was determined that a Marine demo expert would have to be landed on one platform with a satchel full of explosives in order to destroy the platform efficiently. The man did the job right the first time and the platform was destroyed. Other operations are not so risky and graphic but are nevertheless just as tricky.

COUNTERTERRORISM OPERATIONS

Since 1979, when Marine Security Guards stationed at the U.S. Embassy in Tehran were taken hostage by Islamic terrorists, the Marines have developed a serious interest in after-the-fact actions taken by military forces to end a terrorist attack. We already know that

The HK MP5 submachine gun (with silencer) is the primary automatic weapon used by Force Recon counterterrorist teams. Photo by the author.

hundreds of Marines were killed by a single terrorist in Beirut in 1983, a grim reminder that Marines are not invulnerable to terrorism. Marine LtCol. William Higgins was later kidnapped by terrorists in Lebanon and killed after being tortured (he had been serving as a U.N. observer). During this same time, U.S. embassies around the world guarded by Marines came under attack from terrorists, and Marine MGySgt. Donald Goebel was nearly killed by terrorists on two separate occasions while serving as a recruiter in then West Germany in the mid-1980s. Then in the late 1980s, a Marine gunnery sergeant was assassinated by a terrorist belonging to the communist New People's Army (NPA) in Olongapo City, Philippines, and the NPA stepped up its incursions into the Subic Bay naval base there. (This prompted the Corps to send one of its most experienced and capable counterterrorist specialists to the base—then Maj. Ed Miller, a former staff NCO with extensive counterguerrilla experience in Vietnam—to solve the NPA problem. He did so with dispatch by simply showing the terrorists that he could do much more damage to them than they could ever hope of doing to the base and its personnel.) All of these incidents and the continued threat of terrorist action against MEU (SOC) forces everywhere has led to the training and equipping of Marine Force Recon troops and Navy SEALs serving with the MEUs to become proficient in solving terrorist attacks with military force.

Knowing Your Enemy

Profiles are kept not only on individual terrorists, suspected terrorists, and supporters (passive and active) but on the groups themselves. Counterterrorist forces are briefed on them regularly so that they can be prepared to deal with them as the MEU (SOC) operates in a certain group's AO. The modus operandi of each group is studied, which may include bombings, arson, kidnapping, skyjacking, marjacking (maritime theft, such as in the case of the now sunk *Achille Lauro*, aboard which American Leon Klinghoffer was murdered), assassination, extortion, robbery, vehicle theft, and the overt taking of hostages. The structure of the group is taken into account, with attention being paid to the command element (and subcommand elements in the case of large terrorist organizations such as the Palestine Liberation Organization's al-Fatah, Popular Front for the Liberation of Palestine, Hisbollah, and Islamic Jihad), intelligence section, tactical units, and support section. From there the tactical situation is considered and, if ordered by the president, who's in consultation with the Department of State (which consults with the host nation), Federal Bureau of Investigation (FBI), National Security Council (NSC), Joint Chiefs of Staff, Commandant of the Marine Corps (CMC, who is a member of the JCS), and other agencies, a Marine Force Recon Direct Action team or the MEU's SEAL platoon will end the crisis through the application of force (officially known as Crisis Management Counteraction Operations).

The Force

Force Recon platoons deployed with a MEU (SOC) are trained in hostage rescue techniques and other forms of direct action designed to terminate a terrorist attack. The training they receive is continual and ranges from precision shooting with a variety of weapons (e.g., customized pistols, HK MP5 submachine guns, M40A1 sniper rifles) to hand-to-hand combat techniques designed to either instantly incapacitate or kill an opponent. Force Recon Marines attend various schools within the Department of Defense that prepare them for the demands of special operations, such as amphibious reconnaissance, SERE (survival-evasion-resistance-escape), Ranger, Special Forces, airborne, and scuba training. The SEALs serving with the MEU are similarly trained, and Force Recon Marines and SEALs train together regularly. Assorted methods of insertion to the site of the attack can be used, such as closed-circuit scuba (a system that eliminates bubbles by trapping exhaled air), minisubs, and high-altitude low-opening (HALO) and high-altitude high-opening (HAHO) parachuting.

RAIDS

Raids, unlike counterterrorist operations, which the Corps did not put much emphasis on until the 1980s, have long been a part of the normal and frequent operations of the Marines. Small boats and foot marches have traditionally been the insertion methods used in raids. With the advent of the helicopter in the 1950s and the development of effective heliborne raid concepts in Vietnam, Marine raids have grown in diversity and effectiveness. This experience has resulted in raid forces all being task-organized to suit each particular mission, but it has also shown that the same structural organization can frequently be used by all raid forces, even though the exact composition of each may be quite different.

Command Element
The brains of the outfit is centered in the command element and includes the overall commander of the force who controls the movement of the force to and from the objective area and to a degree what happens at the objective. A small but sufficient staff assists the commander with the conduct of the raid from the command post either ashore, afloat, or airborne.

Marines speed toward the beach during an amphibious raid. USMC photo.

Reconnaissance Element

With a three-fold mission, the reconnaissance element reconnoiters the objective area (as well as the route to and from the objective, if feasible), feeds the command element continuous data on what the situation is at the objective area, and provides security for the assault element prior to the main security element taking over from recon once they are ashore.

Security Element

After the insertion of the reconnaissance element and prior to the arrival of the assault element, the security element is inserted and provides security for the assault force while en route to and extracting from the objective area, as well as perimeter security during the actual assault on the objective.

Assault Element

The "meat and potatoes" of the raid, the assault element is the force actually doing most of the fighting at the objective area. It is divided into assorted teams with various missions and responsibilities. For instance, Team McCoy might be tasked with sinking the enemy's patrol boats in the harbor, Team Kimber with destroying the enemy's communications center, and Team Connor with finding and freeing hostages being held in an interrogation center.

Support Element

Fire support is provided by the support element and may consist of mortar and artillery fire, close air support (from attack jets or helicopter gunships), and in some cases naval gunfire. Detailed coordination is required for maximum combat power.

Reserve Element

Even though a raid is offensive in nature, the raid's reserve force is not designed for the exploitation of success at the objective. Instead, the reserve is meant to assist the assault element in case of unexpected resistance. It usually remains afloat until called for.

One of the most precarious decisions that must be made in planning a raid is the number of Marines in the assault element. Where most offensive actions stress the importance of the principle of mass—using large numbers of men to overwhelm the enemy—a raid's assault force is task-organized to utilize the *minimum* number of men needed to accomplish the mission. It therefore becomes more a game of economy of force than mass. Two factors lie behind this: surprise and a planned withdrawal.

Raids use surprise to get the drop on the enemy, i.e., take him unawares. The greater the number of men in the assault force, the more likely detection becomes. And a withdrawal is planned immediately after the mission is accomplished, a facet that allows for fewer men because they do not intend to stick around until enemy reinforcements arrive.

Raid Fundamentals

Raids for the most part are tricky by nature, with many variables that can influence the outcome. This necessitates the formulation of plans that are simple, which is a basic consideration of any offensive action. Everyone, from the raid commander afloat (usually the Commander, Amphibious Task Force, or CATF) down to the rifleman in the assault element, must be fully prepared to carry out his duties.

Communications are crucial, as is the case with command and control, fire support, reconnaissance, and security. Raid rehearsals are a must, and each Marine must be well-versed in all manner of combat skills, from marksmanship to evasion and escape.

Alternate plans must be laid. Fire support must be planned from beginning to end, and gunnery must be available and accurate under all conditions. Reconnaissance teams supporting the raid must provide the best possible data to the command element from beginning to end.

When considering the size of the assault force, casualties must be planned for. A marginally manned assault force at the beginning of the raid will have a more difficult and costly time accomplishing the mission if casualties are taken.

Special Raid Considerations

Currently, the Ground Combat Element (GCE) of each MEU (SOC) consists of three infantry (line) companies, one weapons company (.50-caliber machine guns, 81mm mortars, heavy 40mm machine guns, Dragon antitank missiles, TOW antitank missiles), and the headquarters and service company. Each company is assigned a primary mission for raids, with one taking heliborne, one taking small boats such as CRRCs (Zodiac Marine Commando F470s) or RRCs (modified Boston Whalers), and one becoming the GCE's mechanized company riding in amphibious assault vehicles (amtracs). It is extremely important that each company spend the preponderance of time training for raids in its assigned medium, but it must also have knowledge of the means by which the other companies operate. (This has recently become a shortcoming because of the increased operational tempo of the MEUs and an almost crippling lack of funding from Congress.) This is important because of such operational anomalies as weather which may require that only certain insertion means be used. For instance, the reserve force (experts in heliborne assaults) may be needed to help extract the assault force, which is the small-boat company. Helos may not be feasible due to weather constraints, requiring that additional small boats be launched. If the Marines of the reserve force are not as familiar with the boats' operation as the assault force, the chances of a successful rescue are greatly reduced.

Experienced staff NCOs are the glue that binds the Marines together, and it is they who are responsible for making the training pay off. The proverbial "little things" which might be missed by less-seasoned Marines are caught by the staff NCOs, such as always turning to the left when exiting a CH-53E Super Stallion helicopter so as not to run into the tail rotor on the right; securing weapons to the Marines with "dummy cords" and quick-release knots/Fastex buckles so that, should a boat overturn, they will not lose the weapons; making sure communications and other support gear is secured properly in the bottom of the boat; and making sure the ramp of each amtrac is rigged for a "combat drop" versus having to be lowered hydraulically. They also provide guidance to the commander as to which Marines are best suited for special tasks, such as scout swimmers and snipers, and provide tactical and operational expertise everywhere from the combat operations center (COC) to the assault element itself.

NONCOMBATANT EVACUATION OPERATIONS

NEOs are the bread and butter of the Corps' MEU (SOC) forces and are one of the most common operations performed. The Corps' operational expertise in these often complicated operations began in earnest in 1975 with the evacuation of Saigon and has been fortified with operations like Sharp Edge in Liberia and Eastern Exit in Somalia. Prior to deploying, MEU (SOC) devote many hours to getting these operations down pat.

NEO Categories
NEOs are divided into two categories—permissive, which is an evacuation conducted where no threat is expected, and nonpermissive, which is just the opposite.

A CH-46 Sea Knight lands near the U.S. Embassy in Liberia to evacuate noncombatants. USMC photo.

Permissive NEOs are primarily logistical in nature, with the MEU (SOC) providing medical, administrative, and coordination activities to support the operation with minimal force in evidence ashore.

Nonpermissive NEOs are those that either have the potential for becoming violent or are already so. Riots and other forms of civil unrest, roaming gangs, terrorist activity, and other threats are real, and Marines come ashore in force to perform an array of functions ranging from convoy security and property defense to manning the evacuation control center (ECC) and eliminating enemy snipers with counter-sniper fire from their own snipers.

NEO Units

The advance party forward control element (FCE), command group, security forces, and evacuation control center make up the basic units found within the NEO.

NEOs can be routine—or anything but. USMC photo.

The FCE consists of the officer in charge (either the XO of the MEU or the CO or XO of the BLT), two operations officers (one from the BLT staff and one from the MEU service support group staff), one air officer (normally the XO of the air combat element, or ACE, or the BLT's air officer), one engineer officer, one communications officer or chief (from the MEU or BLT staff), and an intelligence officer (normally the MEU counterintelligence officer). Also included in the FCE is a naval officer, usually a boat group commander or senior boatswain's mate.

The command group's makeup is quite flexible and is determined by the MEU commander. This needs to be so to facilitate task-organization, meaning that the mission will dictate who is in the command group. Once the mission is clear, it becomes easier to decide who should be part of the command group—having the wrong people can be disastrous, and having the right people can be most gratifying and productive. The commander must consider not only *who* to include but how many as well—too few means things can slip through the cracks, and too many means confusion and redundancy.

Security forces are often companies from the ground combat element that serve in a variety of security roles. They may be positioned at landing zones and port/beach facilities, at outlying evacuation points, at assembly areas, or anywhere else they are needed.

The evacuation control center is the key to a successful NEO. Made up of seven sections (headquarters, security, screening, processing, medical, beach/LZ, and transportation), this is where planning and coordination are critical. Nine stations form the ECC:

1) baggage collection
2) registration
3) hold
4) search
5) medical
6) processing
7) screening/interrogation
8) VIP processing
9) release point (to the evacuation site)

There are countless potential glitches in any NEO, and practice for them takes up a substantial amount of the "workups" done by MEUs preparing for deployment. Given the fact that NEOs are one of the most likely special operations the MEU might perform, it is difficult to put too much emphasis on their conduct.

TACTICAL RECOVERY OF AIRCRAFT AND PERSONNEL

Marines use aircraft extensively in their various operations and also employ Navy and Air Force aircraft to support them, as well as Army helicopters from time to time such as those used in the Gulf War. Nowadays pilots find themselves operating in some very hostile airspace such as Bosnia, northern Iraq, and the Persian Gulf.

With an operational tempo that has never been higher during "peacetime," it is clear that from time to time an aircraft is going to either be shot down or brought down by mechanical failure, resulting

This F/A-18 Hornet pilot could easily become the object of a Marine TRAP mission. USMC photo.

in the pilot and/or crew ending up on the ground in a region where "interests inimical to those of the United States" are operating. Classic examples of this would be an F/A-18 reconnaissance flight being struck by an Iranian Hawk missile, forcing the pilot to eject, who then lands in the water and is picked up by an Iranian Revolutionary Guard gunboat; Marines operating in South America being called in to rescue a pilot shot down by narcoterrorists; or an Air Force F-16 pilot on patrol over northern Iraq being downed by an Iraqi surface-to-air missile and captured by their ground forces.

TRAPs are rapidly planned and executed and require quick thinking and attention to detail. Although it is not mentioned in the acronym, the aircraft may have to be destroyed should it be forced down intact in hostile territory. Sensitive equipment may be aboard, and TRAP teams must know exactly what this equipment looks like and where it is located on the aircraft to better assure complete destruction. A thorough briefing along these lines is crucial, and proper training in the use of explosives is required of the team. Should they fail to completely destroy the aircraft and its sensitive equipment, a second mission may have to be launched to finish the job, which is obviously undesirable. This is one of the reasons why first calling in a strike aircraft to destroy the downed aircraft with air-to-surface fire is undesirable, since missiles, bombs, and cannon fire are frequently not as point specific as hand-placed demolitions.

Another facet of the TRAP mission that Marines sometime forget is when the order is given to insert a team of mechanics to fix the aircraft so it can fly out. Marines in the aviation maintenance field do not often contemplate this possibility and should be brought into the training of the TRAP team so that they can become familiar with standard operating procedures of the team.

Options

The commander has three basic options in general when planning for a TRAP mission that does not involve intentional destruction of the aircraft, any one of which could be unfeasible.

The first and frequently most desirable is to plan for picking up any downed crewmen by another aircraft in the flight on the spot or perhaps immediately after the mission has been completed. By not loading all aircraft to capacity, Marines leave room for crews to be picked up. They may also have an empty aircraft along in the flight just for this purpose. Immediate extraction of the downed crew provides the best chance of success.

A second option is to have TRAP aircraft and personnel orbiting or sitting on the deck somewhere near the area of operations waiting for the call. This option is nearly as desirable as the first but takes more time, planning, and assets.

The final and most dangerous option is to insert a "sparrowhawk," which is a team of special operations Marines specially trained to be inserted to recover the crew of a downed aircraft and perhaps destroy any sensitive equipment left intact. This takes time to prepare for and conduct and therefore stands the least chance of success in many instances.

Each of these options must take into account fire support and the possible use of Cobra gunships to hamper enemy activity in the area.

Special Considerations

As a SERE instructor at the Navy Survival School in Maine, one of my duties was to instruct Marine and Navy pilots and other personnel with a high risk of capture such as Recon Marines and SEALs in the proper use of the Isolated Personnel Report Form (ISOPREP). The ISOPREP is a document that is filled out prior to a mission and is kept in the intelligence section. It has special information used by TRAP personnel to authenticate the downed pilot. The information on this document is given to the TRAP team and then used in a question and answer session once the apparent pilot is contacted in person by the team. TRAP team members must understand how this document is used properly, and the importance of having an up-to-date ISOPREP form must be stressed to the pilots, aircrews, and any other personnel who are at high risk of capture.

It must never be assumed that a Marine who has been shot down has a good grasp of land navigation techniques that can be used to get to a certain area or spot for extraction by the TRAP team. I learned as a SERE instructor that some have minimal navigation skills at best, and some have no such skill at all, while Navy and Air Force personnel may have fairly well-developed skills in this area. It goes strictly on a case-by-case basis.

The same is true when it comes to survival and evasion. Many Marines and sailors who fly for a living attend SERE school early in their career and therefore have a basic understanding of survival and evading capture, but it must never be assumed by the MEU (SOC) staff that a Marine stands a better chance of surviving and evading than a sailor, or that a SERE graduate can afford to wait longer to be picked up than a man who has not been through SERE school.

Finally, a special extraction device may be needed to carry out a mission, depending on precisely where the downed pilot/aircrew is located. This may be a jungle penetrator and rescue hook, SPIE rig, or other device, and TRAP personnel must be adept at getting the survivor out with its use. Do not discount the possibility of having to perform a TRAP from the water, either.

• • • • •

Those are only some of the special operations the MEU (SOC) may find itself having to perform. Another possible type of conflict that a MEU (SOC) or other size MAGTF may become involved in is guerrilla warfare. Let's look at it.

CHAPTER 8

Counterguerrilla Warfare

"Guerrillas must move with the fluidity of water and the ease of the blowing wind."

Mao Tse-tung

The terms "guerrilla" and "terrorist" are frequently used as one and the same. However, although it is true that guerrilla forces sometimes use terrorist techniques to achieve an end, many guerrillas do not consider themselves terrorists. Still, according to the accepted definition of terrorism within the Department of Defense and Department of State, any assailant who undertakes "the unlawful use or threatened use of violence against individuals or property to coerce or intimidate governments or societies, often to achieve political, religious, or ideological objectives" is a terrorist, even though America's leftist media often refers to them as "guerrillas" or "extremists" so as not to offend them.

True guerrillas, on the other hand, are the combatants behind an insurgency who do not target noncombatant individuals or property unrelated to defense. Marines have been engaging in counterguerrilla warfare for many decades and at the same time have been deployed against criminal elements calling themselves guerrillas or revolutionaries or freedom fighters or an array of other quaint monikers, such as the Barbary pirates along the North African coast in the early ninteenth century, American mail bandits later on, and hoodlums in Somalia and Haiti as of late. The lessons learned from all these conflicts have helped form the Marines' counterguerrilla strategy.

THE BEST OF THE BEST

Few guerrilla forces have realized the success of the Viet Minh and Vietcong. Gen. Vo Nguyen Giap was one of the latter's most potent sages, and his thoughts on guerrilla warfare are studied in the top U.S. military schools. Although the Corps lost not a single decisive battle to the Vietcong during their tenure in South Vietnam from 1965 until 1973, the government backing the Vietcong still won the war, which is what counts. This war laid the groundwork for the Corps' current doctrine on counterguerrilla warfare.

THE CALCULATING WARFIGHTER

More than any one thing, guerrilla warfare is a war of calculation. Crafty guerrillas, as attested to by Giap, do not engage an enemy on his terms. Rather, they strike when the odds are in their favor and break off the attack and disperse the moment the tide changes to favor their opponent. Three of their most precious assets are their ability to surprise the enemy and do grievous damage to him in a short period of time; remain highly mobile, which facilitates their ability to attack and withdraw quickly under nearly all circumstances; and disappear into the countryside with alarming speed because of their familiarity with the terrain and their usually indigenous nature. An enemy with these endowments is one of the greatest challenges an armed foreign aggressor can face, but it is one that is winnable in most cases. The primary reason why Marines, Navy SEALs, and Army Special Forces were so successful in Vietnam from an attrition standpoint (they killed many more Vietcong and North Vietnamese Army regulars than the enemy did us) was their ability to fight on the enemy's terms; that is, use surprise, mobility, and dispersion to their benefit. The myriad lessons learned by these forces are used as teaching points even today and form the basis for Marine special operations forces' counterguerrilla strategy, namely cold calculation, which is precisely what the guerrillas use so well.

The armchair philosopher armed with a pedantic understanding of the Law of War would be quick to point out here that guerrillas frequently make use of indiscriminate weapons meant to maim or cripple, such as the Vietcong's infamous pungy pit (a camouflaged hole dug into a trail with sharpened stakes lining the bottom and side), where Marines are forbidden from using such devices. But the Law of War does not forbid the use of guile, improvisation, and an attitude of ruthlessness that is tempered with education and a sense of right and wrong. Is the latter a contradiction in terms? No. For a force to be ruthless, it merely must demonstrate that it will not relent until victory is realized, and that in itself is one of the guiding philosophies behind effective guerrilla forces—the belief that their struggle will continue until triumphant.

A SINGLE PRINCIPLE ABOVE ALL OTHERS

Of the nine principles of war, the single most important in counterguerrilla warfare is the principle of the offense. As a nation we failed miserably in abiding by this principle in Vietnam—we failed to get on and stay on the offensive at all levels, and in so doing we constantly allowed the enemy to regroup and re-equip. Marines conducting counterguerrilla warfare operations today focus on the offensive as their means of victory and have no intention of allowing their opponents a moment's rest. Persistence is manifested through gaining and maintaining contact with the enemy and retaining the initiative at all times.

Even when in the defense, a status that every armed force must be in at some point, offensive actions are taken by running 24-hour security patrols both inside, along, and outside the patrol base perimeter.

Offensive patrolling is the best means available in keeping guerrillas on the run. This requires that Marine special ops forces be accomplished in this basic military skill to a degree beyond that of the guerrillas. Emphasis on stealth, communications, and fire support is critical, and units should experience as little personnel turmoil (turnover) as possible before and during the operation. Personnel stability adds to individual and unit familiarities, a desired trait. By living and working with each other for months and hopefully years, Marines get to know one another to such a degree that they can actually know what the other is thinking at times and how each will react to various actions.

Selecting the right man for the job is also important, and sometimes this is best done by just getting out there on patrol to see who has what innate abilities. A few days after being assigned as a recon team leader in a newly formed platoon in the late 1970s, I had to select jobs for my five Marines within the patrol we had been assigned. I assigned Charlie Cordova the point for no particular reason and Stan "The Man" Iramk, a native of the Palau Islands in the western Pacific, as the last man in the patrol, or "tail-end charlie." Five minutes after leaving the patrol base, Stan passed word up to me in my position behind the point man that someone was approaching us from the rear. I gave the signal for everyone to step into the bush and wait for whoever was coming up on us to pass by, but after several minutes no one materialized. Thinking that Stan had seen a wild boar or some other creature and mistaken it for a human, I signaled for the patrol to resume course.

One minute later Stan again passed word up that someone was coming. Again we melted into the black jungle, covered by the dense foliage and darkness. This time I was more patient, and after a solid five minutes a group of men passed by. Knowing that contact from this point on was much more likely to come from the front, I switched Stan and Charlie. I had found my point man in a Marine who spoke very limited English (at the time) but who possessed remarkable night vision, one of the best sets of ears I had ever seen in action, and a way of moving through solid jungle like a specter across a Welsh moor.

Guerrillas operate with the understanding that for them to be tactically effective they must strike weak spots in the enemy's rear areas with surprise, then quickly break contact before he has a chance to react. Marines understand this and have been known to make rear areas appear vulnerable, with few if any rear area security patrols operating. This is a ruse, of course; the appearance of vulnerability is meant to draw the guerrillas into a killing zone covered by hidden, mutually supportive weapons. An unseen mine field may block apparent avenues of approach, with machine guns and preregistered mortar fire creating the desired combined-arms effect. The approach of the enemy can be detected with listening devices camouflaged as vegetation. A quick reaction force may be at the ready to pursue the withdrawing enemy force, and escape routes can be blocked with additional command-detonated mines and preregistered artillery fire.

Offensive actions must be constant and relentless, covering the entire guerrilla area of operations. Imaginative, bold maneuvers keep the enemy guessing as to what you will do next. The villages he has under his control, either overtly or covertly, must be wrested from his hands. A vigorous intelligence collection effort adds greatly to the combat power of the counterguerrilla force and directly bolsters security. Lax security is what the enemy seeks in an opponent, because it is a gap that tends to prove highly effective in crippling the will of the counterguerrilla force. Intense, comprehensive offensive actions are themselves a factor that add to rear area security. If the enemy's AO is constantly inundated with effective offensive patrols whose mission it is to kill every guerrilla who won't surrender and destroy every safe house and enemy stronghold encountered, and those patrols are protected with superior firepower and dedicated fire support, the combat power of the guerrilla force is severely reduced.

HOST NATION SUPPORT

Most counterguerrilla operations are supported by the host nation wanting to rid itself of the insurgency. This support may come in many fashions, ranging from logistical services to combat units assigned to assist the Marines.

Training of host nation forces is paramount to long-term success. USMC photo.

As history tells us, host nation combat forces may or may not be effective. This was precisely the case in South Vietnam, with some South Vietnamese units being crack troops, such as certain Ranger units, and some being utterly worthless, with a bad habit of breaking and running when things got a little dicey. This makes training of the host nation forces a priority.

FORWARD PRESENCE

To best maintain contact with the guerrillas and retain the initiative, it is imperative that Marine special ops forces be deployed and redeployed in positions well forward. This is done by the establishment of secure combat bases as deep in guerrilla country as possible. The risks of such ventures are apparent, but they are outweighed by the advantages made clear through unceasing patrols

Being well forward is a fundamental of maintaining contact with the guerrillas. USMC photo.

and rigorous security measures in and around the combat base itself.

Once a combat base is established, it remains fully operational until the guerrillas in that area are killed, rendered ineffective, or move on to new areas. At this time the combat base should pack up and redeploy to a new position that is again well into the guerrillas' new area of operation. This process continues until the host nation is able to handle the insurgency on its own or the presence of the Marines is no longer deemed necessary for some other reason.

Selecting the site of each combat base is done only after a careful reconnaissance operation, which provides the necessary data for the commander to select the future site. Terrain that is easily defensible is always preferred, but other factors such as resupply, observation, and avenues of approach must be considered, along with enemy operations and special vulnerabilities in the area, host nation wishes, and so on. Hastily selecting a new site for a combat base frequently results in problems that could have been avoided.

Beirut in the early 1980s was a guerrilla war. The MAU commander wanted to establish his base—albeit a "peacekeeping" compound versus a combat base—in the highlands, but was ordered by the White House to take the low ground, largely due to the insistence of President Reagan's national security advisor, Robert McFarland, who, ironically, is a former Marine but was never known as a tactical wizard. The resulting mess underscores the need for good site selection.

● ● ● ● ●

Reconnaissance operations have long provided Marine commanders with the raw data needed to determine enemy strengths and weaknesses. A look at them is in order.

CHAPTER 9

Reconnaissance Operations

"Every move you make, every step you take, I'll be watching you."

The Police
"Every Breath You Take"

T he Marine Corps' reconnaissance community has undergone major changes in the last 20 years. Reconnaissance companies belonging to the Marine divisions, and Force Reconnaissance companies under the command of Surveillance, Reconnaissance and Intelligence Groups (SRIGs), which used to belong to the Force Service Support Groups (FSSGs), have reconfigured themselves to fit a much-changed Marine Corps. In fact, entire reconnaissance battalions like the Second Reconnaissance Battalion once located on Camp Lejeune's Onslow Beach have disappeared and re-emerged joined with the Second Light Armored Infantry Battalion (2nd LAI) to form the current Second Light Armored Reconnaissance Battalion, a mechanized unit specializing in reconnaissance and mobile security for the division and Marine Expeditionary Force. The epitome of clandestine operations, Force Reconnaissance companies have grown from a few platoons specializing in deep reconnaissance to companies also capable of a host of missions in the realm of what is now called direct action. These missions range from the destruction of drug labs to in extremis hostage rescue.

But the *raison d'etre* for reconnaissance units has always been and still is the collection of raw data for conversion into combat intelligence to be used in the decision-making process. Despite the astonishing capabilities of reconnaissance satellites, unmanned aerial vehicles (UAVs), and reconnaissance aircraft such as the venerable U-2 and reemergent SR-71 Blackbird, on-the-ground recon teams usually consisting of between four and six Marines are still the medium of choice for many situations. Because aircraft and satellites can't see beneath a bridge and can't see inside a room, the recon Marine remains the eyes and ears of the commander and provides him with an organic unit dedicated solely to his needs.

THE PIPELINE

In days gone by, each reconnaissance or force reconnaissance unit had its own entrance test. Marines already serving in combat units or undergoing training at Infantry Training School (now known as the School of Infantry) were selected for reassignment to a recon unit only after passing a severe physical and mental endurance test. This is no longer the case. Today the Corps' reconnaissance and force reconnaissance companies conduct a standardized entrance test that, although quite sufficient, is not as demanding as those given in the past. (Suffice to say that these tests were extreme, most of which resulted in less than a 15 percent success rate.)

Marines today are tested for swimming ability and water confidence, physical stamina, mental endurance, and individual motivation in a more controlled and even-handed setting. Those passing the

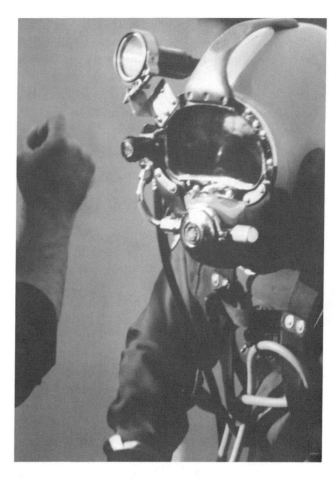

Reconnaissance Marines are fully versed in various diving methods. Photo by the author.

test while at the School of Infantry are sent either directly to a recon unit upon graduation and assignment of their primary military occupational speciality (PMOS) or are first sent to the amphibious reconnaissance course at one of the Corps' two expeditionary training facilities. About two months long, the "amphib recon" course gives the Marine the basic skills needed to function as part of a recon team, with special emphasis on reporting, communications, weapons handling, aquatic and land endurance, demolitions, fieldcraft, and improvisation. The amphib recon graduate is assigned the secondary MOS of 0321 reconnaissance Marine.

This system of taking a Marine directly from the School of Infantry with the intention of making him a recon Marine is called the "pipeline" and is a staffing tool that has reduced the need for recon units to take Marines out of other fleet combat units. However, Marines are still recruited from the fleet through the rank of sergeant.

Once assigned permanently to a recon unit, a Marine's education continues throughout his career. Force recon companies require their operators to be both scuba and parachute qualified, so each Marine is sent to a military scuba school (either one of the Navy or Marine Corps schools or the Army's Special Forces scuba school) and the Army's basic airborne course at Ft. Benning. Additional instruction in special scuba methods such as closed-circuit scuba is conducted at each company, and many of the Marines will take training at the Army's freefall (skydiving) course. Ranger school is also a frequent stop for Recon Marines, as is SERE school, advanced amphibious reconnaissance training, submarine operations, close-quarters battle, sniper training, airborne jumpmaster, advanced demolition techniques, and hostage rescue techniques (taught by the SOTG's Special Missions Branch).

BACK TO BASICS

With the formal addition of hostage rescue missions and other DA actions, the reconnaissance community has become somewhat split as to the focus of training. There are a growing number of experienced staff NCOs within the recon community who want to see less emphasis on these "high speed, low drag" missions and get back to the basics of reconnaissance work, that being clandestine data collection well ahead of the forward edge of the battle area (FEBA). Force recon platoons deployed with the MEUs must now be versed in both disciplines—deep reconnaissance and direct action—to fully exploit the MEU's combat power, and this means that time for training must be somehow divided between the two missions. The question has been posed: can you really have a unit this small that is able to perform both missions very well?

The Navy and Army both think not and have separate units (SEAL Team Six and whatever they are calling Delta Force these

Recon Marines frequently are cross-trained as snipers. Photo by the author.

days) to accommodate their special needs. This leaves the Navy with several other regular SEAL teams to perform underwater demolition and reconnaissance and the Army with Ranger and Special Forces units to perform its missions. The Marines, on the other hand, only have Special Missions Branch at their SOTGs, and these tiny units do not deploy with the MEUs. Should the Corps train a separate unit for deployment with the MEU whose sole mission is to perform direct action? The jury is still out on this, but it seems quite unlikely to happen in the near future.

THE RECON MISSION

Ground reconnaissance can take two forms: visual and audio, the latter of which involves the planting of acoustic sensors, usually delivered by aircraft, into the enemy's AO to determine his whereabouts,

Reconnaissance Marines were the first ground forces to witness the burning Kuwaiti oil fields. Photo by the author.

movement, strength, and possibly equipment. Visual ground reconnaissance is done by Marines on foot in the enemy's AO, who seek to learn of the enemy's whereabouts, strength, disposition, distribution, and composition. Also, information is sought on terrain features, vegetation, and structures of all types (runways, bridges, roads, supply and fuel depots, staging areas, communications facilities, command and control facilities, natural resources, fortifications to include obstacles, etc.). This information is all collected surreptitiously with the aid of photographic equipment, field sketches, and other means and is used to determine both enemy strengths and weaknesses, especially the discovery of gaps in his defenses.

Reconnaissance is done not only along the enemy's front but all along his axis as deep as possible. By providing up-to-date information on what is going on in the enemy's rear without him knowing about the surveillance in a timely manner, the commander is better able to direct not only the actions of strikes against the enemy but can conduct actions along his front as well.

Deep reconnaissance is best done with Force Recon Marines who are trained and experienced in the craft. However, reconnaissance to the immediate front of an advancing unit need not always be done with Recon Marines per se—infantrymen can be employed effectively in this task, as can scout-sniper teams organic to the MEU and the simple manning of strategically located observation posts. These measures, when linked with UAV flights, sensors, and other reconnaissance measures will suffice if employed wisely.

DOING THE JOB

The first rule of ground reconnaissance, when the mission calls for clandestine movement to and from the objective as well as undetected actions while there, is simply one of stealth. Recon Marines must be extremely adept at moving about and doing their job with complete secrecy while at the same time retaining the ability to maneuver quickly (which frequently means scampering away from potential trouble and hiding in some dank and uncomfortable place until the danger has passed). To facilitate this, the very best insertion and extraction methods must be used, and the technical and tactical abilities of each team member must be beyond reproach. Each man must be able to operate a Global Positioning System terminal; be fully versed in the operation of all team communications equipment; take useful photographs and draw detailed terrain sketches; be a superior marksman; be capable of completing the mission on his own should the remainder of the team be killed; be an expert navigator with map and compass; have the ability to travel long distances over land or water at a strenuous pace with all his weapons and equipment; survive

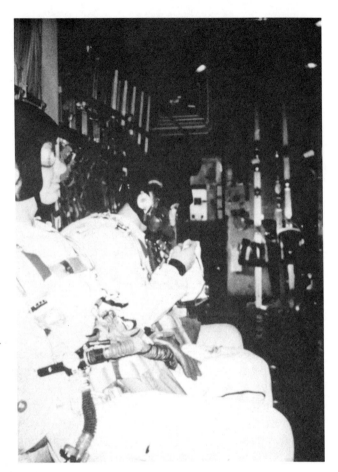

High-altitude low-opening parachute insertions are a common method of insertion for recon Marines. GySgt. R.L. Weaver, USMC, photo.

and evade capture; and be able to do countless things in order to accomplish the mission at all costs.

Given this, recon Marines always orient on the enemy unit, terrain, or other feature to be reconnoitered. This entails certain risks that are normally accepted, as this is the nature of reconnaissance, not the least of which is a loss of close proximity to friendly units. This is the primary reason why stealth is so important in reconnaissance—should the recon team be discovered and taken under fire, they may not have a friendly unit nearby to help them, and fire support may not be available due to weather constraints or other priority fires.

Reconnaissance patrols seek to locate the enemy as far ahead of friendly units as possible so that the commander can use information relayed back to him as far in advance as possible. This makes dependable communications equipment and methods crucial, with immediate reporting of information being routine. Recon teams must not wait until the entire mission is complete and they are on their way back to friendly lines before readying reports and transmitting information; such a delay could cost the maneuvering unit dearly. And the team must be highly knowledgeable in what to look for while reconnoitering an enemy unit's position, finding gaps and gathering information that will help the S-2 (intelligence section) determine the enemy's combat power and particular weaknesses and vulnerabilities.

Reconnaissance units use unusual tools to accomplish their mission. Photo by the author.

OBJECTIVE CONSIDERATIONS

Reconnaissance missions focus on commander's intent, i.e., the supported unit's mission. His intelligence and operations staffs advise the reconnaissance unit leaders (who in the case of a MEU [SOC] force recon unit would normally be a captain and a gunnery sergeant) of the objective and then consult with them about how the MEU's objective can best be supported. Details of what the commander needs to know are brought out, and thus begins reconnaissance mission planning. As the plans are laid, priorities are established, time lines laid, reporting procedures ironed out, etc., and special attention is paid to time constraints. The deeper and more detailed the mission, the more time must be allowed for completion of the mission (which includes extraction of the team). Frequently more than one team will have to be inserted so that multiple missions can be accomplished simultaneously or close to it.

Of acute importance is the method of both insertion and extraction, with timely mission accomplishment being key. The commander must avoid unnecessarily dangerous methods of getting the team in and out, and he must select the method that maximizes the likelihood of success. However, should the recon leaders advise a method that is hazardous but clearly the best available—parachute, scuba, etc.— every effort must be made to support that advise.

BASIC MISSIONS

There are three basic types of reconnaissance missions: area/point, route, and zone. The mission of the supported unit dictates which type of recon mission is assigned.

Area/Point Reconnaissance
When the commander needs to know some specifics about enemy activity in a certain area or perhaps about a certain feature (bridge, village, ford site, etc.), an area/point mission is assigned. This means that the commander believes that accurate, detailed information about that area, feature, or object is critical to the success of the

overall mission, i.e., the commander's intent. This makes it absolutely imperative that the recon unit not be detected or suspected while en route to, at, or withdrawing from the area/point.

Route Reconnaissance

Route reconnaissance is a very common recon mission that surveys potential routes for the supported unit. Many factors are studied, such as the supported unit's ability to control key terrain features overlooking the route, choke points that might be used as ambush sites, obstacles, roadway limitations, etc. Stealth is important because an enemy covertly observing the actions of the recon team can easily determine what they are doing out there and in many cases will be able to set up an ambush along the route with relative ease.

Zone Reconnaissance

When the commander needs a large area reconnoitered that is defined by boundaries of some sort (natural, cultural, or implied in relation to the operations order), he directs the reconnaissance unit to perform a zone reconnaissance. Usually this entails gathering information on anything and everything within that zone and therefore takes time. Placing multiple recon teams operating within the zone at one time is standard in order to hasten the collection of data.

•••••

That's a look at reconnaissance. Now let's move on to the danger zone.

CHAPTER 10

The Danger Zone

"The principle of annihilation is the fundamental law of war."

General Waldemar Erfurth
Surprise in War

R egardless of the nature of the war, the battlefield is fraught with danger. Uncertainty, risk, and chance await the combatant at every turn, it sometimes seems. How danger is handled by the individual Marine can have a clear influence on the outcome of the battle or may simply become a hair-raising sidelight in the annals of the fracas. The latter was the case in late February of 1991 when Fox Company 2/4 assaulted its final objective of the Gulf War.

Up to this point, Second Battalion, Fourth Marines, or "two-four," had been performing pretty standard stuff: clearing trenches holding Iraqi soldiers and destroying a variety of vehicles with our TOW missiles and other assets, our radios frequently carrying the familiar, calm, almost casual voice of the battalion commander, LtCol. Kevin A. Conry, orchestrating the attack. On our final night in the attack, the seasoned battalion was assigned the mission of capturing the United Agricultural Research Facility (UARF) in the Kuwait City suburb of Al Jahrah along the 6th Ring Road, a superhighway. Intelligence told us that a brigade from the Iraqi Third Armored Division was operating in this area, and we noted on the approach that armored resistance was increasing as we approached the facility.

Shortly after nightfall, our night vision scopes filled with the sight of the UARF, and we were rather surprised to see not desert but tall pine trees looming up on us. This sprawling complex, we were about to learn, was surrounded by a tall cinder block wall and covered with greenhouses, a vineyard, cattle and horse pastures, various agricultural plots, and something more sinister—a warren of Iraqi bunkers. The area was criss-crossed with dirt and asphalt roads linking these bunkers, which were made of sheet metal, concrete, cinder blocks, timbers, and other materials. Fox Company 2/4 was about to leave desert warfare and begin something altogether different.

Fox Company was assigned the task of capturing the portion of the facility situated along the highway and above a dairy farm just shy of an overpass with the mangled hulks of several Iraqi armored vehicles scattered about. The company's amtracs pulled into the complex, and we quickly dismounted to begin the daunting task of clearing each and every bunker, some of which were completely underground and some of which were only partially so. This meant that each bunker was going to have to be taken a little differently from the previous one.

This area, it became clear, was divided into two sections: one consisting of bunkers that served as living quarters and the other made up of bunkers holding all sorts of ordnance, including SA-7 Grail surface-to-air missiles, Sagger antitank missiles, small-arms ammunition, hand grenades, rocket-propelled grenades, tank rounds, and assorted other ordnance. When the ammunition caches were discovered, the word was quickly passed that our standard method of clearing

A Marine of Fox Company holds Polaroid photos of an Iraqi soldier's family found inside a bunker in Al Jahrah. Photo by the author.

bunkers—tossing in a hand grenade, waiting for it to detonate, and then storming inside—would have to be canned; a grenade tossed into a bunker filled with ordnance might very well explode and kill all the Marines nearby. Now we would have to enter each bunker without the preliminary grenade.

As the company was clearing the bunkers, I studied my map and location, noting that the highway was a great avenue of approach that an Iraqi counterattack force coming from Kuwait City could rapidly advance down to our position. I called for Sgt. Joe Negron, my mortar section leader, and told him to lay the mortars along the dirt road we were on to cover the highway "danger close," referring to the close proximity of the target area (the distance from the dirt road to the highway was about 130 yards) and in a parallel sheath. He responded in a clearly pissed-off tone that he was already in the middle of doing that and that I should not try to do his job. (NCOs have a way of taking offense when they think you are trying to do their job and do not automatically assume that they are doing what they should be doing without being instructed to do so.) As he stalked off into the gloom, my radio crackled with the voice of 1st Lt. Paul Racicot, the weapons platoon commander, who informed me that the company commander, Captain Schlaepfer, wanted me to get the mortars laid along the dirt road I was standing on to cover the highway in case of a counterattack. Naturally I responded in a pissed-off tone that I didn't need the CO trying to do my job. Secretly I was happy that we were all thinking along the same lines only a few seconds apart—the sign of a good team.

To add to our perimeter defense, several M1A1 tanks were brought into our position and emplaced so that their 120mm main guns were facing up and down the road. As they slowly made their way through our position, the whine of their turbine engines made us feel much safer and very superior—the queen of the battlefield was with us, and I realized then just how the hapless Iraqis must have felt seeing these great steel beasts rumbling across the sands toward them.

Perhaps miraculously, no one in Fox Company was wounded in this part of the operation, although I did manage to wound myself by hastily exiting a bunker with my head just a little too high, finding a crossbeam in the darkness (I had taken off my helmet to hear better). Despite the potential for danger that evening, the following day would prove even more hair-raising.

Fox Company's limit of advance was the knoll overlooking the dairy farm about half a mile down a slight slope toward Al Kuwait (Kuwait City). On the final day of the war, the battalion had been ordered to hold its position in the UARF and allow the Arabic Coalition forces consisting mostly of Saudi, Kuwaiti, and Egyptian soldiers to pass us by and take back the capital, which was being evacuated by the Iraqis. (Those same Iraqis were about to be caught on the highway running from Kuwait City to the Iraqi city of Basra in a murderous onslaught conducted by aircraft from the Third Marine Air Wing and tanks from the Army's tough Tiger Brigade, which was positioned along Mutlaa Ridge. The infamous road would become known as the Highway to Hell, Highway of Death, Carnage Road, and Death Valley, all fitting monikers that attest to the folly of the Iraqis. This surreal scene of absolute mayhem was created by not only many dozens of Iraqi military vehicles decimated by Marines in the air and sharpshooting soldiers in tanks and Bradley Fighting Vehicles but an equal number of Mercedes, BMWs, and other luxury cars that had been stolen by the Iraqis in Kuwait City.)

Looking down upon the dairy farm, I could see no signs of Iraqi activity. I could see no activity at all, for that matter, except for some cows milling about. I then made a decision that to this day I have no rational explanation for: I decided to reconnoiter the farm—alone.

Strolling down the hill feeling very superior with my M16, I came across the bloated carcass of a huge Holstein cow that had met its maker, apparently about a week earlier given the stench. To my right was the farm itself, consisting of the main farmhouse, several outbuildings, a large barn or two, and a dirt driveway that ran up to the house and split a pair of large holding pens that were crammed with cows. I noticed that the cows were filthy and in desperate need of milking, their udders greatly distended. As I walked up the driveway they began to low, perhaps hoping that I had come to milk them. Their mooing sent me ducking behind a barrel, my rifle trained on the door of the farmhouse should any tardy Iraqis be hiding therein and come out to investigate why the cows were making a racket. After waiting for a few minutes I decided to continue my approach.

Approaching the open front door at an angle, I could see two Arab headdresses and a pair of olive drab trousers hanging from a clothesline running between the house and an outbuilding, and I wondered to whom they belonged. I could not see inside the house, but I listened for a few moments for any activity inside. Hearing nothing, I then decided for reasons I will never know to just step into the doorway.

On the dirt and tile floor about 3 feet inside the house was a tray holding three cups of steaming tea. It was at that precise moment that my brain actually engaged and I thought, you dumb son-of-a-bitch,

Newman. There are Iraqis hiding in here and here you are half a mile from your company with only your rifle, a few hundred rounds, and some grenades. You're an idiot and deserve whatever you get.

One second later a man stepped in front of me from out of the shadows of the house's interior, an AK-47 in his hands.

In the next millisecond I dropped to one knee as I brought my rifle up to my shoulder, flipped off the safety, and aimed directly at his chest. I looked at the man and determined that he wasn't an Iraqi but a farmer, for he was dressed in gray trousers, a white long-sleeved shirt, and a gray and green sweater vest. He has no idea how close I was to emptying an entire magazine of ammo into his chest.

I indicated to him that I wanted him to put the rifle down, which he happily did while smiling in his best smile that showed his well-spaced, brown teeth, and he then launched into a barrage of Arabic mixed with hand and arm signals that obviously meant he wanted me to sit down on one of the tattered chairs outside and have a cup of tea with him. I obliged after checking the house for anyone else, and the

The farmer himself. Photo by the author.

farmer commenced to tell me in Arabic and sign language the tale of his farm being captured and occupied by Iraqis and of their hasty departure yesterday (I gathered) as the Marine armored assault approached. He was obviously in need of some food and water, so I excused myself after drinking the hot, sweet tea and listening to his story in order to go back to the company and get some water and MREs (meals ready to eat) for him.

Once back at our position, I told the company first sergeant, Rick Buchikos, what I just found, and he and I grabbed some cases of MREs and a few liters of water and humped back down the hill to the farmer, who once again launched into his tale.

THE CHEMICAL AND BIOLOGICAL THREAT

In January 1991 we were informed of some of the tricks Saddam's henchmen were attempting in Kuwait, one of which was the opening of the oil spigots at the terminals around Kuwait City's harbor. This was intended to create a giant oil slick—and it did—which Saddam hoped would float south and foul the desalinization plants along the Persian Gulf coast of Saudi Arabia. However, this crafty albeit despicable attempt to strike one at the Coalition Forces' water sources proved futile. I despised this crime against nature but admired the Iraqis' resourcefulness.

This was an indicator of the lengths to which the Iraqis would go to defeat us, so it came as little surprise to us when we looked to our north one evening just below the Saudi-Kuwaiti border to see hundreds of oil wells burning intensely in the Wafrah oil field. This astonishing sight led us to believe that the warnings we had received about Saddam's intent to use chemical and biological weapons against us were founded in fact, and we all checked our chemical protective gear for the umpteenth time before getting into our amtracs for the assault through the berm, obstacle belts, and mine fields. While looking at the ghastly inferno to the north, I recalled that three weeks earlier, Fox Company had walked straight through an animal graveyard in northern Saudi Arabia and found the desert floor covered with partially buried animals of all kinds—dogs, sheep, goats, camels. I wondered what had killed them all and how they came to be where they were and considered for a moment that they might have fallen prey to a chemical or biological weapon, but I had no proof of this whatsoever—it was just a thought.

Despite the United States government's constant claims that no chemical warfare weapons were used by Iraq during the Gulf War, the Marines have documented their use. One proven attack came at 0656 on 24 February when a vehicle from the Second Marine Division's Second Assault Amphibian Battalion struck an Iraqi mine containing a blister agent. Two Marines who were not fully dressed in chemical protective gear were wounded, with nasty blisters appearing almost immediately on their exposed skin. Close by was a Fuchs "Fox" vehicle, which is crammed with sensitive and very accurate chemical detection equipment. It instantly sounded a warning, and the entire Second and First Marine Divisions went to MOPP (Mission Oriented

An Iraqi gas mask lies where its owner left it in northern Kuwait, a sign of what plans the Iraqis had in mind for us. Photo by the author.

Protective Posture) Level 4, which means full chemical protective gear was to be worn until further notice.

Later that same day at 1116, the Army fired off a message to all commands that it had positively identified anthrax in dead sheep found near King Khalid Military City. I wondered once again just what had killed those dozens and dozens of animals we had traipsed through a few weeks earlier.

Four years after the war, as an instructor at the Staff Noncommissioned Officer Academy at Camp Lejeune, I interviewed a student who was with Task Force Grizzly in the Gulf War. One of his jobs as a recon platoon sergeant was to perform crater analysis at the conclusion of Iraqi artillery barrages, and as part of the analysis he would test the crater for chemical agents while in full protective gear. His equipment announced that lewisite, a blister agent, was present. This was one of the agents and delivery means used by Iraq during its recent war with Iran.

The hundreds of burning oil wells from Wafrah in the south up through Burgan in central Kuwait to Maqwa in the north were also concerning us, especially after the cessation of hostilities. Second Battalion, Fourth Marines was the last Marine combat unit to depart Kuwait (May 1991), and the battalion had maintained its position along the Sixth Ring Road in the United Agricultural Research Facility since the final day of the war. This position was just west of the burning Maqwa oil field, and every few days the winds would shift to blow out of the east, which sent the oil smoke our way. On many occasions you could not see your hand in front of your face at high noon. Our hootches and vehicles were covered with a fine, oily sheen, and our uniforms began to deteriorate. The word came down from division headquarters that during these times no one was to do any strenuous physical activity and that if possible everyone should remain in their tents and hootches until the wind changed once again and shifted the smoke.

A Navy medical team showed up one day, and I ran into an experienced Navy doctor whom I had met the year before at SERE school. She took me aside and told me that they were concerned about the long-lasting effects of the oil smoke and "other things" we had experi-

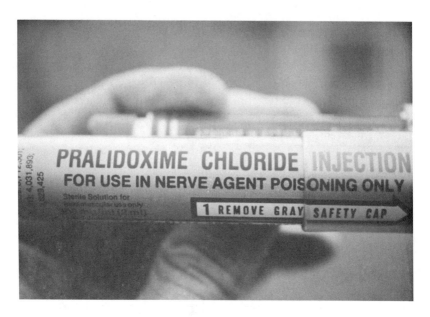

The author's nerve gas antidote injector in the Gulf War.

enced and that I should keep a close watch on my health and that of my men over the coming years. Less than a year later I found a strange rash spreading down my face that took doctors three years to get under control. They call it Gulf War Syndrome, and many of the Marines from 2/4 have similar or much more serious problems, ranging from unexplained birth defects in their children and still-born babies to short-term memory loss, severe weight loss, and chronic fatigue.

Danger comes calling in unexpected ways on the battlefield.

CHAPTER 11

Sleight of Hand

"Lead flew everywhere, but you could not see the enemy, only his fires."

Capt. Roger L. Pollard, USMC,
after his light armored vehicle company was attacked
by an Iraqi armored column at an observation post
in northern Saudi Arabia, resulting in two of his
vehicles being destroyed by friendly fire, one of the
most costly Marine engagements of the Gulf War

D eception is one of the oldest and frequently most devastating of combat multipliers. By using trickery, legerdemain, ruses, and other tactical sleights of hand, an armed force that is by far and away numerically, logistically, intellectually, and physically inferior can suddenly gain the upper hand and win the day. Deception can be used by any size force, from the individual reconnaissance Marine evading capture 20 miles deep in enemy territory to the Marine Expeditionary Force.

Even ill-equipped and -trained forces such as the Iraqis knew and used deception to draw attention away from weapons and activities they wanted to remain secret. I recall coming across what appeared to be an Iraqi artillery position in the desert, which was in reality a large hole with a 55-gallon drum lying in the bottom of it, upon which was propped a long piece of pipe covered with camouflage cloth. From a distance it appeared to be a howitzer and drew quite a bit of fire until it was enveloped by a squad of Marines and "captured." The Iraqis who emplaced it were long gone, of course.

Deception is a game of influence, where the force attempting the deception wants to influence its opponent in some way. This may be in order to make the enemy commander do something they want him to do or perhaps make him avoid some action that will impede the perpetrator's progress. Basically, there are seven reasons why Marines undertake tactical deception.

1) *To gain time.* Although speed is often critical on the battlefield, conditions may require that the Marines gain time in order to better evaluate the situation. They may even trade space (terrain) for time if it suits their needs.

2) *To surprise the enemy.* Numerically inferior forces can quickly achieve victory by surprising the enemy in a place and at a time when he least expects it. This is a principle that Marines rely upon to gain the upper hand over an enemy who far outnumbers them.

3) *To gain information.* Tactical deceptions, when and where properly and cleverly employed, can help determine the enemy's strengths, weaknesses, disposition, composition, and intentions. Knowing and understanding the enemy means everything on the battlefield, and this is one means of achieving that end.

4) *To exhaust the enemy.* By making the enemy think that the main attack or some other worthy target is happening somewhere, Marines can exhaust or severely deplete the enemy's ammunition and will to fight. Drawing fire where it really isn't needed is an ancient ruse still very applicable on the modern battlefield.

5) *To force action.* A tactical deception can cause the enemy to move forces away from what the Marines intend to be the primary focus of effort. This is best seen as a classic supporting attack that makes the enemy think one thing when another is going on behind his back.

6) *To reduce combat power.* Any advantage the enemy might have—superior numbers, weaponry, or the occupation of key terrain— can be reduced insofar as combat power goes by using a deception.

7) *To protect what you have.* In the defense as well as the offense, cunning can reduce the Marines' losses and therefore preserve their combat power for use at the decisive time and place.

DECEPTIONS

There are four basic types of tactical deceptions, any of which might be used by a MEU (SOC) or other MAGTF.

Demonstration

When a Marine force is used to engage the enemy at a particular place and time in order to fool him in some way, but with no decisive engagement by that force being expected, you have a demonstration. Seldom (if ever) is contact even made. A force being used as a demonstration must be large and "loud" enough to convince the enemy that what he is seeing is the real McCoy and not a trick of some kind to draw his attention away from something going on elsewhere.

A classic example of a demonstration involved the Marine forces afloat in the Persian Gulf during Operations Desert Shield and Desert Storm. As the ground war began, the amphibious assault ships steamed closer and closer to Kuwait in an attempt to make the Iraqis believe that an amphibious assault was imminent. The Iraqis shifted forces from a southerly orientation to an easterly one, creating a gap to the south that was exploited by the Marines in the northern Saudi desert. Of course, the Marines at sea never came ashore.

Feint

Feints always include an engagement, but with limited objectives that aren't expected to prove decisive. The true objective—the decisive one—is brought under attack by the main force located elsewhere. This is especially useful when concealment of the main attack is absolutely crucial to the success of the operation. Like a demonstration, the feint must be orchestrated so that the enemy is convinced that it is the main attack.

The Iraqis used multiple feints on the evening of 29 January 1991 when they attacked two outposts along the Saudi-Kuwait border to get our attention, then struck at the port city of Khafji and took it almost without a fight. Of course, we took it back immediately and beat the hell out of them for fooling us like that.

Display

Displays can be very intricate and fall into one of four categories—disguises, portrayals, simulations, or combinations of any of these.

MAGTFs of all shapes and sizes can alter gear, positions, and weapons to make them appear to be something other than what they actually are. For instance, a light armored vehicle (LAV) can be disguised to look like a tank by strapping a piece of pipe onto it (simulating the main gun).

Portrayals are more complex. This is when a unit tries to convince the enemy that it is some other unit or a unit which doesn't even exist. Electronic emissions are one means of helping to make the enemy think the way the Marines want him to think.

Simulations are meant to make the enemy think that such and such exists in a certain area when in reality it does not. This deception is the most complex to orchestrate effectively and can take quite some time to set up and pull off. A fine example is how entire "units" were created in England—complete with tanks, planes, artillery, and all the other trappings of a major assault force—prior to the Normandy invasion during World War II. Of course, all that gear was fake, constructed of rubber, paper-mâché, wood, and other materials, and made to look like a real unit staging its gear.

Combinations of any of these deceptions are possible in some cases, and the commander who uses his imagination can achieve great success.

Ruse

No one can possibly know how many ruses or tricks have been perpetrated upon an enemy that resulted in a battle or perhaps even a war being won. In its simplest form, a ruse is a form of psychological warfare in the form of a lie or some sort of misinformation designed to make the enemy believe something, such as a certain unit is to be moved from here to there or that an attack will take place at a certain time and place and be conducted by a particular size force. The trick is to make it appear as though the information the enemy has come by was done so quite by accident while not making it appear too good to be true.

MAKING THE MOST . . .

Marine Air-Ground Task Forces, especially the smaller ones like Marine Expeditionary Units and Special Purpose MAGTFs, must make the most of limited deception resources. This means that planning a deception along one or more avenues—electronic, sonic, olfactory, or visual—must be done with the utmost care and resourcefulness. But when planned and conducted so that various deception measures complement one another, the results can be impressive.

Electronic Emissions

By broadcasting phony radio messages and emitting other types of electronic signals, the Marine special ops unit can convince the enemy of countless things, running the full gamut from possible future intentions to the movement of genuine units. The level of sophistication must be appropriate for the enemy the deception is intended for—too simple a scheme will warn an advanced enemy and too complex of one will be indecipherable to a third world force with limited or no experience in this arena.

Visual

Visual means of deception are as varied as the circumstances in which they can be employed. At night, lights can be used to make the enemy believe that a large unit is operating at a distance. During daylight hours, everything from camouflage and smoke to reflections and dummy materiel and facilities can be used.

Olfactory

Smells such as diesel fumes and food odors can be used quite well, especially at night when lights are being used to convince the enemy that something is happening to his front. As is the case with visual deception techniques, the weather and terrain play a role in the effectiveness of the ploy.

Sonic

Particularly useful at night in many cases, sounds meant for the enemy to hear can be used in conjunction with lights and perhaps odors. Diesel fumes sent toward the enemy from hidden drums of burning diesel fuel and an assortment of loud vehicles with their lights on can often convince an enemy that something is afoot. Mix in the sound of ammunition being fired and you can have quite a show.

• • • • •

At this point we need to take a look at a facet of warfighting that Marines fail to consider in many cases—the defense.

CHAPTER 12

For the Defense

> "Positions are seldom lost because they have been destroyed, but almost invariably because the leader has decided in his own mind that the position cannot be held."
> MajGen. A.A. Vandegrift, USMC
> *Battle Doctrine for Front Line Leaders*

T he Marine Corps has never been known as a force with extensive experience in the defense, because since the Corps' very inception it has been employed as an offensive force meant to strike quickly and decisively and then withdraw. Still, there are a few classic examples of how Marines can defend well, such as the Peking Legation during the Boxer Rebellion, the garrison on Wake Island during World War II, and the fire base at Khe Sanh during the Vietnam War. On the other hand, the Marines were in the defense when they were handed one of the most horrific defeats

A Marine amtrac dug into the northern Saudi desert forms part of Fox Company 2/4's perimeter defense in February 1991. Photo by the author.

in their celebrated history with the bombing of the Battalion Landing Team's headquarters building in Beirut, the act of a single man. This event served to awaken the Marines and show them that reputation isn't everything, and that every armed force must at some time go into the defense, regardless of how distasteful a proposition it is.

Of the two, defense is naturally stronger than the offense when that defense is a deliberate one. This is so because the defender is able to select terrain of his choosing to defend and therefore selects the battle position he intends to fight on. The enemy on the offensive must come to him, and this is a tremendous advantage that can be likened to your defending your house from an intruder who you know is coming and who has never been in your house before. You know the "terrain" better than he does and have had a chance to prepare for his arrival. You can channel him into areas where he can easily be killed and can even watch him as he approaches and thus shift your defenses to cover the avenue of approach he has selected.

WHY DEFEND?

It has been said that one defends when he is weak and attacks when he is strong. This is generally true, with one exception being the defender who sets into the defense in order to cause the enemy to attack when that enemy isn't fully prepared to do so—in other words, to present the enemy with a target he just can't resist that appears vulnerable but actually isn't as vulnerable as it looks, and at a time when the attacker isn't as strong as he would like to be. But, generally speaking, the defense is assumed for any of seven reasons:

1) To retain a certain piece of terrain while gaining time

2) To prevent the enemy from controlling indirectly (through fires) or actually occupying a certain piece of terrain

3) To provide logistical support, i.e., resupply

4) To develop greater combat power

5) To improve the situation for future offensive operations

6) To economize on forces

7) To lure the enemy into a trap

Still, even a deliberate defense can crumble when not planned and executed with vigor. On the evening of 29 January 1991 at an observation post manned by a reconnaissance platoon along the Saudi-Kuwaiti border, an Iraqi armored assault materialized out of the night and attacked the outpost. The recon platoon's position was defended by a company of light armored vehicles (LAVs), which had set into the berm should any Iraqis show up. The company commander, however, did not anticipate a bold offensive maneuver by the Iraqis, which resulted in the observation post nearly being overrun as the Recon Marines engaged the tanks and infantry fighting vehicles with automatic weapons and M66 LAAW (light antiarmor weapon) rockets at extremely close range.

In the resulting confusion, one LAV was destroyed by another LAV that had fired a TOW missile, killing the entire crew. The company commander was having difficulty seeing the Iraqi vehicles and called in air support. Two A-10s showed up and Dash-1 (the first aircraft in the attack) dropped a flare so that Dash-2 (the second aircraft) could see the Iraqis and fire. The flare was dropped short, however, and landed near the LAVs. Dash-2 fired and obliterated another LAV, killing seven Marines. The Iraqis eventually withdrew, but the damage had been done. The Marines had learned yet another lesson about preparing for the defense.

History tells us that many battles lost by defenders were the result of those defenders giving way to the attacking force, yet there are examples of defenders giving ground only to reorganize and counterattack at a decisive time and place. But for the most part, you should stay the course and gut it out, such as the Marine defense of their fire base at Khe Sanh during the 1968 Tet Offensive in Vietnam.

One means of adding to the defense's combat power is the use of concentric and ever-increasing volumes of fire as the enemy approaches the main battle area (unless the defensive plan calls for an ambush close in). This means that fields of fire must be cleared well forward of the main battle area so that long-distance weapons such as naval gunfire, artillery, TOW and Dragon missiles, and mortars can be employed to reduce the enemy force as it comes on and perhaps to channel that force into areas it cannot maneuver in so easily. As this is going on, the defender must always be alert for gaps in the attacker's forces that can be exploited to further reduce his combat power, initiative, and resolve. At the same time, the defender must quickly employ his counterattack force to deny the enemy the chance to exploit any successes he may achieve.

DEFENSIVE FUNDAMENTALS

As in the offense, fundamental rules apply to the defense. In this case there are 10 basic principles that help guide the special operations Marine commander in setting into the defense.

Surprise

Yes, this offensive fundamental is also a defensive fundamental, and as we will see in the next few pages, there are quite a few similarities between the offense and the defense.

Surprise can be achieved in the defense by allowing the enemy on the offensive to be drawn into an ambush. The effectiveness of the ambush has been clearly demonstrated to the Marines in their past, especially in Vietnam where the ambush was a favorite defensive tactic of the Vietcong. If the situation indicates that an enemy force might be deceived into believing that it has indeed found a gap in the Marines' defensive perimeter—explaining why it did not come under the usual concentric and ever-increasing volumes of fire—it can be ambushed in close. The key is to get as large an enemy force as possible into the kill zone and then eliminate the soldiers as rapidly as possible using horrendous volumes of fire and the combined-arms concept to put them in a dilemma, i.e., they have no place to run. Selecting the right place and the right weapons is crucial if this is to work.

Surprise will be of limited use unless the combined-arms effect is brought into play, and the defender planning an ambush must always be prepared with an option and never assume that his plan is perfect. For instance, a commander might make the mistake of registering artillery and mortar fire in a kill zone and leaving evidence of this

The infantry company's assault section can be employed to quickly destroy enemy armor and other vehicles in an ambush site. Photo by the author.

fact—craters, shrapnel, and other clearly visible effects. An alert enemy point man moving toward this kill zone will pick up on these signs and inform his leader, thus avoiding the ambush.

Preparation

No defense is truly invulnerable regardless of the time and effort devoted to it by the defender. However, preparation is essential and goes a long way toward increasing the combat power of the defender.

The defender who sets up in a deliberate defensive position (a situation where the defender has time to fully prepare his position) must

Preparation includes communications, as this Marine messenger on his Kawasaki motorcycle can attest. Photo by the author.

ensure that each primary fighting position is backed up with an alternate fighting position from which the Marines manning that position can carry out their primary assignment should the primary position become untenable or its effectiveness reduced. Also, a supplemental position for each Marine must be established should their original plan go bad and a gap be discovered by the enemy. If time permits, an alternate position for that supplemental position should also be made.

Maneuver

Maneuver in the defense? Absolutely. There are two types of defense: area (also known as static and position) and mobile (occasionally called dynamic). Maneuver is involved in both but to a larger degree in the mobile defense.

A mobile defense is based around a defensive position where terrain and fire are employed together to destroy an attack. It can focus on permitting an attacker to access an area which he does not know is

This Iraqi vehicle clearly was not used properly in the defense. Note the gaping hole in the door.

Photo by the author.

a kill zone and upon his entering that area using a very powerful mobile reserve to wipe him out after he has engaged lighter defensive forces placed in the forward area of the battle position. Although originally conceived for large units such as Marine divisions, this tactic can be employed effectively at the regimental level and on occasion at the battalion level when special conditions permit. A substantial depth to the defense is required for this type of defense, which explains why larger units normally use it.

The area defense is quite different from the mobile defense. Here the majority of forces are forward and prepared to defend a selected battle position without the use of a strong mobile reserve to exploit success. Terrain that strongly favors the defenders and an enemy that is especially strong are two factors that point toward an area defense. In the area defense, the reserve force is used to counterattack any enemy penetrations, restore the battle position, and reestablish depth to the defense that may have been lessened by successful enemy maneuvers.

Mutual Support

Like interlocking fields of fire, mutual support in the defense refers to the ability of two separate units both set in the defense to assist the other when one is attacked. This is best done when the supporting unit does not have to relocate or maneuver, but this isn't a prerequisite. However, the supporting unit must consider the fact that the enemy may be trying to dislocate it, thus making it vulnerable. Marine special ops units understand that the enemy may try to trick one unit into supporting another and therefore, whenever possible, set up in the defense so that deceptions such as this can be recognized and dealt with accordingly.

Concentration

Another offensive fundamental that cross-decks to the defense, concentration in the defense is used at points and times judged critical in the eyes of the commander. In the defense, concentration must be focused on those points and at those times where and when the defender believes the attacker will assault. This is not an easy task in most instances.

Terrain, known enemy nuances, weather, and many other more subtle factors all affect the decision-making process of the enemy. The wise defensive commander takes all of these into account and plans accordingly. Artillery, mortars, close air support, mine fields, and long-range automatic weapons (as well as snipers eliminating selected priority targets) are all used to concentrate fire in vital areas at a time most disadvantageous to the enemy.

As in the case of supporting attacks in the offense, economy of force is essential when it comes to concentration. The lion's share of combat power must be focused on the enemy's main effort, with the remaining defensive forces being reserved for the counterattack. The wrong decision along these lines by the defensive commander will likely result in his position becoming untenable.

Offensive Actions

In the defense, an aggressive commander continually prepares his forces for offensive action regardless of the reason behind his assuming the defense in the first place.

Though the deliberate defense is truly more powerful in nature than the offense, it is offensive action that is the most decisive—few wars are won through defensive actions as a whole. This principle is best applied in the defense by using counterattacks (which like any offensive action always contain not only a scheme of maneuver but a plan of supporting fires) against enemy penetrations through gaps created in the perimeter, maneuvers designed to spoil or thwart enemy attacks that are still in assembly areas or other vulnerable spots, and actions that otherwise reduce the combat power of the attacker prior to his reaching the point and time that he has determined to be decisive.

A highly mobile and vigorous reserve sent against penetrations immediately after the enemy's initially successful rupture of the perimeter can be devastating to the attacker and crush his will and resolve. Likewise, spoiling attacks conducted while the enemy is still in assembly or staging areas tend to be very demoralizing and serve to reduce combat power in future operations. And harassing attacks, deceptions, and other ruses that reduce the attacker's combat power prior to his arrival at some critical juncture will only further reduce his effectiveness on the battlefield, thus allowing the defender to resume the offensive and take the battle to the enemy.

Knowledge

One of the oldest and most potentially destructive precepts in warfare is knowing your enemy. It holds as true today as when Gen. U.S. Grant fell back for a second time against the Rappahanock River and split his forces again to come back against General Lee in one of the most outrageous defensive maneuvers ever performed, greatly hastening the end of the Civil War by crushing Lee's army in the heart of Dixie. Grant knew that Lee would never expect this manuever from him. He who truly knows his enemy can anticipate him, and the combatant who can anticipate his opponent has a window to his enemy's mind.

During the Gulf War, the Marines knew that they were facing an experienced enemy who had just come through a long and very grueling war with their blood enemies, the Persians (Iran). Like the Army, the Marines studied that war at great length in order to determine the Iraqis' strengths and weaknesses. We knew that they tended to set up in a defensive perimeter that took on the shape of a triangle and that they favored the use of artillery and air power to reduce the combat power of their opponent. We also knew that theirs was not a decentralized philosophy of command, and that they had badly overextended themselves insofar as mutual support and logistics were concerned. This gave the Coalition forces two tremendous opportunities that were translated into distinct advantages—local commanders were reluctant to act on their own, and the forward-deployed forces were extremely susceptible to being cut off from friendly forces and resupply. Gen. Norman Schwartzkopf capitalized on these facts greatly and instructed his forces to exploit them to no end, turning loose Marine LtGen. Walter E. Boomer and his I Marine Expeditionary Force to run rampant over horrified Iraqi forces in Kuwait, while highly mobile and aggressive Army forces conducted a deadly envelopment up through Iraq. The results are history.

Flexibility

Inflexible defenses like the Spartan phalanx at Leuctra lend an often fatal sense of unassailability to the defenders. (The victorious

Thebans were fluid and flexible, while the Spartans were rigid.)
Conversely, the best defenses are those that are fluid in design and merciless in retribution. Flexibility is made possible by excellent reconnaissance measures being conducted continually and a deep and accurate knowledge of the enemy's ways and means. Planning in a flexible defense means due consideration is given to not only those maneuvers the enemy is deemed most likely to use and those avenues of approach believed probable but also those maneuvers and avenues of approach that seem distant. Remember that the enemy with a solid grasp of the fundamentals of the offense will not conduct those maneuvers he thinks you will be ready for and will not utilize those avenues of approach he feels you will be waiting along. Instead, he'll try to find some seemingly minor gap in your defenses and exploit it with enough speed and concentration to overwhelm you at a time and place you did not expect. Arrogance on the part of the defender has been the cause of countless defeats.

Defense in Depth

The final defensive fundamental is nonetheless critical. By defending along the entire defensive axis, the defender is able to wither the attacker's combat power over both time and terrain, absorbing his hopeful penetrations until they are enveloped through fire and maneuver and cut off from forces meant to exploit their success. This causes the attacker to strike the same spot again and again rather than seek gaps elsewhere. By doing so, he becomes predictable and therefore vulnerable to whatever combat power the defender can bring down upon him.

Defense in depth destroys the attacker's momentum (one of the fundamentals of the offense) and thus begins to allow the defender to dictate terms to the enemy. When that momentum is lost, the attacker may decide to reestablish that momentum by committing his reserve, a pivotal mistake if the defender exploits it by using the combined-arms effect and maneuver to force the attacker to break off his assault and withdraw. (In the attack, reserve forces are used to exploit success as opposed to failures and shortcomings.)

Above all else, the defender's willingness to defend his position even when small arms, close combat, and hand-to-hand combat are brought into play is often the one indeterminable factor that causes the defeat of the attacker. Photo by the author.

• • • • •

Both the offense and defense are tangible in nature. In conclusion we must look at the intangible, which is a major component of combat power.

CHAPTER 13

Combat Power

"In war the chief incalculable is the human will."
B.H. Liddell Hart
as quoted in *Encyclopedia Britannica*, 1929

I n my offensive tactics and maneuver warfare classes, I discuss combat power at length. Unlike tactics, the principles of war, offensive and defensive fundamentals, and logistical concerns, combat power is based as much in the intangible as the tangible. A classic example of this is the Gulf War, where one of the largest, most well-equipped, and experienced armies in the world was thrashed at the hands of a hastily assembled multinational force that had never before been configured together. How the Coalition won this war, a war that will no doubt be studied by tacticians

A Marine staff NCO brushes up on his warfighting knowledge at Camp 15 in Saudi Arabia a few weeks prior to the ground war by reading Sun's The Art of War. Photo by the author.

and strategists for centuries to come, was through a complete and clear understanding of the principles behind combat power. Let me explain.

First let's look at the leadership philosophies and generals involved. Saddam Hussein and his senior officers had set up a military with a strictly centralized philosophy of command, whereas the United States military, in particular the Marines with their 9-to-1 enlisted-to-officer ratio, was set up with just the opposite—a decentralized philosophy of command like that of the German army in both world wars. Iraqi commanders did not enjoy the same freedom of thought and action that American commanders did. This resulted in little if any initiative on the part of local Iraqi commanders, while American commanders were encouraged to think and act on their own.

The top brass of the American forces consisted of some very impressive and seasoned individuals. Gen. Colin Powell, USA, the Chairman of the Joint Chiefs, recognized the perfect soldier to place in charge of the war, that being Gen. Norman Schwartzkopf, USA, a bona fide leader of men and tactical wizard who had the will to win at all costs and knew how to do just that. (General Schwartzkopf would later describe the Marine assault into Kuwait as "brilliant.") LtGen. Walter E. Boomer, USMC, was the commander of the I Marine Expeditionary Force and also commanded the U.S. Marine Forces Central Command, making him one of the Corps' most experienced generals. In charge of the Marine divisions were MajGen. James M. Myatt, USMC, running the First Marine Division, and MajGen. William M. "Bulldog" Keys, USMC, running the Second Marine Division. Major General Keys was largely credited with the overall strategy behind the Marine Corps' tactics during the ground war.

All of these generals had reputations for turning their forces loose, with instructions to do as they saw fit, and that is precisely what happened. This policy resulted in the Americans being able to immediately gain and maintain contact with the enemy, quickly and continually develop the situation, and seize the initiative at virtually every turn. In short, the Iraqis simply could not keep pace.

Second, let's look at the overall tactics. In short, the Marines attacked up through Kuwait while the Army performed what amounted to a giant, extremely complex single envelopment through Iraq. Air power had been kicking the devil out of the Iraqis in Iraq and Kuwait both and continued to do so during the ground war. The Iraqis were extremely vulnerable in every instance, and the phenomenal speed of the Army attack into Iraq and the Marine charge up through Kuwait stunned the Iraqis to a degree seldom witnessed in so short a time frame.

Third was the matter of superior technology. Up against "smart" bombs that chase targets designated with lasers and bombs that are guided through a tiny TV camera in the nose of the weapon, cruise missiles that can literally fly through an open window if so directed, and attack aircraft that are all but invulnerable to attack from the ground and air, the Iraqis stood no chance of defending themselves. No chance.

Fourth was the leadership provided at all levels, from the fire teams up through the divisions. Today's Marines and soldiers are taught leadership skills throughout their careers and are both tactically and technically proficient to a level desired since the end of the Vietnam War. They knew how to lead, fight, and win.

Fifth was national resolve. It was clear from the start in August 1990 that America was behind her military in this one. This knowledge was instrumental in the "can do" attitude of virtually every unit. It was amazing to see what armed forces can do when they believe they are right and know that the people back home whom they are doing the fighting for appreciate them and their selfless actions.

All of these things add up to combat power, but they are not the only components. There is no complete list of the things that make up combat power, for there are too many subtleties involved.

A SHORT LIST

Combat power is the full measure of strength an armed force can muster against an enemy. It includes but is in no way limited to:

1) esprit de corps
2) personal and overall resolve
3) the effectiveness of weaponry and tactics at all levels
4) superior logistical procedures and capabilities
5) leadership techniques
6) training
7) knowledge of the enemy and the wisdom to use it wisely
8) the moral support of the nation

The day before my unit crossed the line of departure in the Gulf War, I gathered my Marines together to give them some last words of advice while I contemplated our combat power and the task ahead.

"Listen you hoodlums. I don't want any unnecessary goddam heroics and other weird stuff like that. I promised all your wives and girlfriends back in the world that I would get you back safe and sound and in more or less one piece, and I aim to do just that. Now, we're gonna cross the LOD tomorrow and do some serious whippin' up on these scumbags, and to do that all you have to do is remember your training and cover each other's butts. You are the best platoon I've ever had, and I know you guys are going to do very well in combat.

Believe in yourselves and the reason why we are here. There will be one hell of a party when we get back. Now go forth and kill, and remember that 'no matter where you go, there you are.'" (The last is a quote from the movie *Mad Max—Beyond Thunderdome*, which struck me as being rather amusing. My platoon just snickered.)

I knew that I had done everything in my power to prepare them for the rigors of combat; they were a good platoon and were part of a good company that was part of a highly respected battalion led by a professional officer. I suspected that our combat power was pretty damn impressive and would be proven correct in the coming melee. It was the most gratifying feeling I have ever experienced to see my Marines in action functioning like the proverbial well-oiled machine.

• • • • •

In the preceding chapters we've traveled far, covered a lot of ground. Let me finish up by reiterating that although I have shed a lot of light on Marine special operations and expeditionary warfare in general in this book, I do not pretend to be the originator of such philosophies as the fundamentals of the offense and defense, the principles of war, and so on. These things were born long before my time and will be around long after I am gone. What I do hope I have done is make them a little clearer, a little more personal. If I have accomplished that, then I have done my job as I intended it to be done when I conceived of this book.

Semper Fidelis.

About the Author

M arine Gunnery Sergeant Bob Newman enlisted in the Marine Corps in January 1977. He served his first infantry assignment with Third Battalion, Third Marines, which at the time was part of the First Marine Brigade in Kaneohe Bay, Hawaii. Since then, he has served in numerous billets, including reconnaissance team leader (parachute and scuba qualified), water safety-survival instructor (WSSI), survival-evasion-resistance-escape (SERE) instructor at the Navy SERE School in Maine, weapons platoon sergeant during the Gulf War, and company gunnery

GySgt.
Bob Newman

sergeant. He is currently a warfighting instructor and squad advisor at the Staff Noncommissioned Officer Academy at Camp Lejeune.

Bob's military education includes the Staff Noncommissioned Officer Academy Advanced Course, Basic Airborne Course, Navy Scuba School, Submarine Escape Trunk Operator Course, Navy SERE Instructor Course, Water Safety-Survival Instructor Course, Warfighting Program, Formal School Instructor Course, Infantry Operations Course, Dynamics of International Terrorism Course, Revolutionary Warfare Course, and various other formal schools.

Bob's deployments have been with the 31st Marine Amphibious Unit and 24th Marine Expeditionary Unit (Special Operations Capable), with assorted fly-aways to the Far East, Middle East, and Caribbean, and the Second Marine Division in the Gulf War.

Bob is the author of numerous books, including *Wilderness Wayfinding* (Paladin Press, 1994), and thousands of newspaper columns and magazine articles on outdoor skills. He is the founder of L.L. Bean's Outdoor Discovery Program's Wilderness Survival Workshop.